It's Better To Believe

JOHN D. VERDERY

It's Better to Believe

Published by
M. Evans and Company, Inc., New York
and distributed in association with
J. B. Lippincott Company, Philadelphia and New York

To D. B. A.

CONTENTS

Introduction

The circumstances under which I attended my first Sunday school class were unusual. For one thing I was the teacher, and for another there was a policeman in the back of the room with a billy club to keep discipline.

For the presence of the policeman and his club the explanation was simple enough. The class was being conducted in a reform school. This particular one housed its boys in a series of cottages, organized according to age and previous records and current behavior. Most Sunday school classes in most cottages did not have policemen; mine, however, was named Reception. It contained what in a more conventional type of boarding school would be called "the new boys," and so little was known about them that it seemed wise to have a policeman with a club in the back of the room. Had the authorities known that the teacher was himself a new boy, they might have had two policemen, each with a club.

How I, the teacher, happened to be such a greenhorn is a much more complicated story, involving not only

Introduction

me and my family but the whole history of religion in America from the turn of the century. Since a lot of people know more than I do about that sweep of history, and since it only indirectly has anything to do with this book, I shall touch simply on what seemed to affect me.

As small children, my sister and brother and I never went to Sunday school or church. The reason, I was somehow vaguely and indirectly led to believe, was because my mother had had religion jammed down her throat by *her* mother when she was a child. So she revolted, never went to church, and neither did we. However faulty her reasoning at that time, at least she did not commit the crime of "sending" us to Sunday school.

When we were about half grown up, my mother suddenly "got religion," and as suddenly we all started to go to church. We were living in Greenwich Village in New York at the time, and the church was the Episcopal Church of the Ascension, at Fifth Avenue and Tenth Street. The rector was the Reverend Donald B. Aldrich, and my mother was one of many hundreds of people who fell under the spell of his very reasonable and exceedingly winsome faith. I fell under it too. He was my boyhood hero, the hero of my young manhood, and has continued to be the hero of my later years. Even long afterward when he became my father-in-law, an association which is proverbially supposed to leave little room for hero worship, he remained my hero. This book is not about him, so I shall resist the temptation to digress. I only say now, because now is the proper moment, that except for him this book would never have been written. Through him I "got religion" and so rushed off to reform school to teach it to others.

Introduction

Thereafter my religious development was noted for its ever increasing movement toward orthodoxy and for that reason doesn't make such interesting reading. Perhaps, seen against the background of the religious history of our time, it was more orthodox all the time than I suspected. My grandmother must have been a lot like other people's grandmothers in those days, and my mother—both before and after her conversion—a lot like other people's mothers. Also, along with countless others, I discovered the church during wartime, and heartily agreed with William Thomas Cummings' famous pronouncement: "There are no atheists in the foxholes." Religious fashions change, and I guess my family changed more or less according to schedule.

Only now do I begin to find myself lined up with an ever decreasing minority. People are still going to church, to be sure, and I am kept busy. But there are many indications that there are new religious fashions in the offing, that they are not very orthodox, and that a lot if not all of the old ideas "have simply got to go." I feel as though I am about to be left at the post. So perhaps it is a little in the spirit of nervous self-defense that I write—though I like to believe from firm personal conviction as well.

The question is, in all the changing fashions from my grandmother's time to mine, to my son's, to any future grandson's, is there anything that has always been and will remain valid and relevant? Of course I think there is. And I think this abiding quality is most often found, however long a particular generation may have allowed it to lie dormant, within the bounds of formal faith.

This book is written twenty years after my ordination to the Christian ministry. All of that time has been

Introduction

spent as the headmaster of a church-related boys' school. It has been, therefore, a kind of peripheral ministry, bringing me in contact with a greater variety of people of varying degrees of religious commitment than most clergymen encounter in their work. Among the men with whom I have taught, the boys we have taught, and their parents and friends, there has been almost every degree of churched and unchurched, cynic, skeptic, doubter, and believer. My observation has been—and this is what this book claims to be about—that no matter what the question, no matter what the situation, it is generally a little bit better handled by someone who believes than by someone who does not. So I have concluded that it is better to believe.

Of course everyone believes something, but I mean here to be more specific. By belief I mean a more or less clearly articulated, specific, historical faith, such as my grandmother, my father-in-law, and even I, in my late limping way, have professed. This faith need not have any one name to the exclusion of all others, but it must be historical, since I believe that tradition, properly defined, is an important vessel of truth. I am a professed Christian and write openly from that conviction, but I believe that the point could as well be made from the standpoint of any other historical religious position.

The chapters which follow vary greatly in subject matter and tone. Some of them are not openly religious at all. But all of them intend to say the same thing. It is better to believe. Faith works.

The reader will find no closely reasoned theology. I am no theologian. Besides, theology has to do with validity. My concern is with efficacy. Of course I be-

Introduction

lieve the efficacy of faith is admissible evidence of its validity. But that is merely a personal conviction of mine and not the subject of the book. If the reader shares it, I am glad. However, that is his business.

The selection of topics has been admittedly arbitrary, partly because for my purposes I am not sure there is any better basis for selection and partly because it is consonant with my thesis that any example, any human problem, any question, any dilemma, will prove the point as well as any other. If what follows still seems to some to be a potpourri, I can only argue that the name of the pot is faith.

Death

I begin with death, not because it is so dark and fearful but because it is the background for light, a grandparent of faith even though at times, like many ancestors, it can be an embarrassment to the family. I shall consider its mystery and confess its seriousness without succumbing to its reign of terror. If it is always better to believe, then it is never better to believe than when coping with the fact of death. It is a special blessing of the faithful that here indeed they are able to cope better than most. And clearly, the greater one's faith the more successfully does one cope. I do not believe death is the final test of faith, except chronologically. But it is a severe test and brings many things into focus for a man's soul.

Death seems a proper point of beginning too because it is universal. No one can pretend he is not interested or that it is no concern of his. One can appear to be callous on the subject for a time but not forever. So not very many people deny their concern. Even children ask questions about death almost as soon as they are able to talk, the same questions, incidentally, which they go right on asking for the rest of their days. Of course there are those whose interest is merely academic or even frivolous, but probably this attitude is a pose and certainly it is temporary. So it would seem to be safe to assume that to start with the subject of death is to solicit the attention of everyone, however much that attention may vary.

Whether the approach is intellectual or emotional, whether subjective or objective, whether a person is faced with the loss of one close to him or the end of his own life, I believe that the question and the situation are both handled somewhat better by those who have some sort of clear and formal and historic faith than by those who do not—other things being equal. (And perhaps now is a good time to acknowledge that other things are not always equal, so that a man without faith but with courage, or without faith but with a naturally phlegmatic temperament, or without faith but with a born graciousness of spirit, may indeed confront a difficult situation more impressively than someone else with faith but without some of these other gifts. I would argue, however, that each of these other gifts is always enhanced by faith, even though it does exist among the less faithful.)

There are, I think, three frames of reference from which death may be considered: death in the abstract, a kind of philosophical or theoretical consideration of a phenomenon; the actual death of someone other than one's self, presumably one much beloved or very close; and one's own death. Of the three the first, naturally, is the most neglected. As I have already said, it is not wholly neglected, but for reasons having to do with fear, uncertainty, insecurity, superstition, and sad memories from the past, most people avoid thinking about the subject or discussing it as much as possible, until it is forced upon them by the fact. Death, as a subject for speculation or general discussion, is about as common today as was talk about sex in our grandparents' day.

This is a pity. It is a pity partly because a freer discussion of the subject, by its very universality and ultimate nature, would inevitably shed light on other allied subjects—like life and meaning and purpose. The ancients understood many things which we understand less well today just because they were not afraid—because of their faith—to wonder, out loud and to themselves, about death. Without waiting always for death to confront them, they would occasionally confront it, finding, of course, some advantage in such initiative.

It is a pity, too, because a little thought about death before it is pressed upon us might prepare us better to meet it when it is. Most sensible parents prepare their children for the initial experience of school long before it happens, as well as for puberty and college and marriage and even taxes. But death is seldom discussed except in a whisper or a whimper just after it has happened or when it is knocking at the door. So the words rumble by, "I am the resurrection and the life, saith the Lord: he that believeth in me, though he were dead, yet shall he live: and whosoever liveth and believeth in me, shall never die." To the unprepared, they are meaningless and powerless, at best a genteel convention and at worst an invitation to bitterness.

I do not think it is mere coincidence that the only sensible things I have ever heard or read on the subject of death, except in the atmosphere of imminence, have been spoken and written by believers. Only they, for example, seem to have the courage to face its finality squarely, without either cringing or indulging in flights of frivolous fancy about the Happy Hunting Ground. (It is amazing in such a sophisticated society as the United States how persistent is the theology of the American Indian on this subject!) However unspecific his convictions about the hereafter may be, at least the believer does not confuse it with the here, which he recognizes to have an end, a finis, a final moment. In short, through his faith he has had the courage to face the fact of his finitude, without trying either to gloss it over with juvenile sentimentality or escape it by running away.

The believer also, having contemplated death on his own time, so to speak, has managed to answer some questions by saying, "I don't know." And more important, without being in the least guilty of any lack of curiosity, he has been able to add, with dignity, "I don't need to know."

Of course no one is ever ready for death, in the sense of being wholly prepared, any more than anyone is ever ready for marriage. But I do believe that the contemplation of the subject by a man of faith, from time to time throughout his life, makes a difference. A friend I once knew had occasion to minister to hundreds of people at the point of death or in sorrow for others. His own death was heralded by an inordinate number of warnings and close calls over a period of years. Through his faith (a very orthodox faith in God) and faith in people and faith in the essential goodness of life, he was able to face his own last days with a courage so great it appeared more as a blithe spirit than as a grim determination to be brave. After he had taken three trips to the hospital in ambulances, with heart attacks, he once said to me, "You know, I suppose one of these trips must be the last. I really can't expect to come back *every* time." "Blessed are the meek," said Jesus. The French word for meek is "debonair," suggesting a lightness of heart about everything, including one's own very existence. When this man joked about his own death, he meant it. He was not whistling in the dark. He was laughing in the light, the light of his own faith.

The most common frame of reference for the consideration of death is the death of a friend or associate or loved one. Rarely does a man have to face his own death without first having made its acquaintance through the death of others. How hard it hits, of course, depends upon how close one was to the person who died. It can hit pretty hard. The pain can be next to unbearable. When it is, then it is the pain itself which rules the heart. There is a kind of selfishness about this pain, so extreme that it even presumes to forgive itself its selfishness. And so does the rest of the world, though for an astonishingly short time. Conventions about mourning vary from a few days to a lifetime. Both extremes must be wrong, but each suggests a truth. It is true that one ought not, and practically and spiritually cannot, indulge one's self in sorrow for very long. It is also true that death *is* permanent and the loss absolutely irreparable. The American widow who, within a month or two of her husband's death, courageously sells the house and moves to something more economical and goes out to get a job, perhaps her first, recognizes the former. The French peasant woman who

Death

dresses in black for the rest of her life attests to the latter. Both are right, and both are wrong. Each in her way is being realistic and each in her way is pretending.

But in any case the pain is good. Without it one might go all through life without ever having one's heart made sensitive to any ultimate questions. The most saintly men of religion throughout Christian history have kept themselves saintly and spiritual largely through their capacity to take to heart the death of Jesus Christ, as though it had just happened. This does not mean that they have been perpetual mourners, but they have mourned, and so they have been comforted—comforted not just about the death of Jesus Christ or about death itself, but about all the perplexities of life. Without any such vast capacity to preserve sensitivity of spirit for a lifetime, almost everyone achieves something of the same for a little while whenever he experiences the death of anyone close to him. How long it lasts depends upon many things, and one of them is faith.

My own first serious brush with death came at the death of my mother when I was twenty-two. To me the blow was devastating, the loss staggering, and the pain so excruciating that I wondered many times how I could bear it. Then one day the pain receded. The sudden realization of that fact staggered me almost as much as the death itself. Instinctively I began to long for the pain to return, to experience horrible feelings of guilt when I got through a whole day without pain. I remember with what horror I realized one night just before going to sleep that I had not given my mother a single thought all day long. To some degree, I believe I was right to be so upset. I am sure now that the pain was good, for from it there was much to learn.

Death

Consciously to recall such pain through prayer is, I think, the duty of the faithful, a duty handsomely rewarded with an extra touch of grace to the soul.

Eventually, however, the pain must largely pass. This too is natural and proper. Life is change and part of the change is death. Time, though overworked as a solution to all problems, is relevant here. And with time one gains perspective.

Perspective, as I shall have occasion to reiterate more than once, is a primary gift of faith, and nowhere is it more needed and more helpful and more difficult to achieve than in the face of death. Through faith one can at least pretend to see things as God sees them, to see, for example, that pain must be, then that it is good, then that it is terribly personal, and at last that it is indeed a little selfish. Who am I to complain? Standing under the stars on a bright, clear, moonless night, far from home, looking up, one's loneliness or sorrow is assuaged by the realization that the same stars shine on loved ones and on strangers and on strangers' loved ones. And the rain too falls on the just and the unjust. God must have a lot on his mind. Who am I to complain? How did the tradition develop that heaven is above us? No one knows, but it seems right to look up. It is from the heights that one sees best, and faith lifts a man up, high enough so that he can even look down on himself. Is that what I look like to God? How small am I! Who am I to complain?

A good and not very old man lay at death's door, as it turned out with only a day to live. His wife, brave and confused, asked the traditional question, "Why, why, why?" One could argue that there was much to be thankful for. He *was* a good man. The world had benefited by his presence on it. He had, until his last days, suffered very little and enjoyed much good fortune. But it was no time for argument and so the question persisted. The only answer is, "I don't know. But I guess God knows what he is doing." If you can believe that, you don't really have to understand. What is needed is not always comprehension but rather acceptance. After all, if you believe there is a God, you must believe He has wisdom beyond our ken. Strangely and suddenly, the wife seemed to understand, or at least to submit with no bitterness.

A young married couple had a very sick five-year-old daughter. After months of anguish she seemed suddenly to recover, then as suddenly she died. There was anger and bitterness in the hearts of her parents, understandable and human, like the outcries of Job. They blamed God and rejected Him. He had played them a dirty trick. But the God they blamed and rejected (so well-known to Job) was in fact a stranger to them. It was rather like rejecting in high dudgeon the "friendship" of a casual acquaintance. Unlike the ancient Hebrews, they were not able to reconcile a good God and an unhappy fact. Such can be reconciled only by faith—a faith strong enough to say, no matter what, "Thy will be done."

At the outset I suggested that the emphasis of this discussion was to be on the *efficacy* of faith, not so much on its nature; nor was it in any way to be a plea for a particular faith. But here I feel constrained to stress again what I mean by faith. I mean something traditional and historic. I mean a church religion. I mean a pattern of regular worship—public and private —of a *personal* and *living* God. It is on this basis that the young parents of the dead child referred to above were, in my opinion, found wanting, or rather, un-armed. There will be reason to return to this point later on. But for the moment, I want only to clarify what I mean by a believer and to discuss the difference be-tween the more faithful and the less faithful.

Once I conducted a funeral service for a young man who had died without ever having had any particular religious convictions or pattern of life. His mother, however, was a most faithful churchwoman, simple in her belief, but firm and clear. It was to me, in very selfish terms, the most wonderful funeral service I have ever conducted, simply because I realized, as I read on, that she believed every word I was reading. "I am the resurrection and the life, saith the Lord: he that believeth in me, though he were dead, yet shall he live: and whosoever liveth and believeth in me, shall never die." True! True! Of course! And "who *shall* sepa-rate us from the love of Christ?" In my attempts to comfort that woman I was comforted. The words sop and opiate, so often used by skeptics and cynics to describe the validity and function of religion, are ter-ribly loaded words. If we say that religion is strength for the weak or medicine for the sick, we say funda-mentally the same thing—without the skepticism and cynicism. Surely religion is these things. But who is strong? And who is never sick? The real question is, is it strength enough, does the medicine work? I say yes to both of these. And that's enough.

The third frame of reference from which death may be considered is one's own. In some ways, strangely enough, one's own death is easier to accept than the death of a loved one. Or perhaps it would be more

Death

proper to say that it is easier to avoid accepting the thought. The fact is that everyone knows he is going to die but nobody believes it—except in moments of crisis or very near the actual end. So one can philosophize and banter more or less lightheartedly. Every life insurance salesman would be a millionaire if it were not for the fact that most people, most of the time, just don't believe that death is for them .

But we cannot pretend forever. The older we get, or the sicker we get, or the more honestly we face and consider the fact, the more we must come at last to reconcile ourselves with death. This reconciliation is no easy test of a man's faith; perhaps it is the most difficult of all, though I am not sure. Certainly there have been many men whose faith has been sufficient to carry them through every crisis of life except this last. And here they have faltered. When such is the case it is sad, though no one who has not been there is in a position to find fault.

What we shrink from is finality, for our very selves, this time. Whatever may be our convictions or our superstitions or our wistful thinking about a hereafter, we know that the end of life on earth is indeed the end of something. And whether our lives have been happy or sad we almost always try to hang on to what we've got as tenaciously as we possibly can. In this tenacity is revealed how we fear a final period at the end of the sentence of life, our own life.

For the faithful, of course, it is no different. Neither here nor elsewhere do I mean to imply that people of faith have not the same struggles, the same frustrations and fears and gnawings at the soul as those without faith. I merely maintain from my own acquaintance with the faithful, that they handle the situation better. They too shrink from death's finality. But, according to the measure of their faith, it seems to me that with their loins girt about with truth, they face the fact more squarely, more bravely and also with a lighter heart.

Though touched perhaps with a bit of fiction, I love particularly the account of the death of Sir Thomas More in that remarkable play *A Man For All Seasons*. In the last scene, Sir Thomas walks calmly up the steps to the scaffold where he is to be beheaded. As he walks, there is some banter between him and the mob. Someone asks him what makes him so sure that he will see God in the hereafter which so immediately confronts him. As he kneels before the block, Sir Thomas says whimsically—and they are his last words, "He will not refuse one who is so blithe to go to Him."

In our tenacious desire to hang on, one thing which I believe we all too often fail to see is that our wish to live forever (which we express simply by saying to Death, "Not today, please. Come back some other time.") is not only futile. It is also wrong. God made us finite. He intended that there should be a limit. He means us, I am sure, to accept death not only bravely but honestly and with not too deep regret. So did Jesus of Nazareth on the cross when he said, simply, "It is finished." There were tears, but they were not his tears.

We can believe that what He said He said without scorn, without bitterness, without sorrow. One can detect perhaps even a kind of reverence for death. I believe God hopes that all men will die thus, facing its order of finality squarely, even, as Jesus did, going to meet it.

In the light of this finality there are, of course, im-

Death

plications and reflections about life. The first is that death is a warning—a necessary warning. We do not have all the time in the world. How much we have we do not know—perhaps another hour, perhaps a year, perhaps fifty years. We do not know. But we do know there is a limit. "The days of our age are threescore and ten," wrote the psalmist some three thousand years ago. Actuaries today tell us we live longer, but we still do not on the average improve much on that ancient figure.

And so, if our life is to have meaning when it is finished, we must get on now with the job of filling it with meaning. The hope for immortality is a proper Christian hope and includes the possibility that some things can be redeemed beyond the grave. But the life here and now stands for what we have made of it here and now. There can be no retroactive infusion of meaning into what may have been meaningless. So by death we may be warned. The time is now or never. Even the Son of God had not all the time in the world. "The Word became flesh and dwelt among us." The Word is still among us, but not the flesh. The flesh was for a time, a very short time, and what was to be done had to be done before that time was up. So at last the flesh had nothing left to say except a kind of simple signature. "It is finished."

It shall be thus for the rest of the world as well. We know it, though we do not always live as if we knew it. Too often, too much like drunken sailors we squander the time of our lives. Death is the inexorable day of reckoning, when such squanderings appear at last indelibly on the balance sheet. Death is a warning, and for it as such we may be grateful.

Death

That death is also a blessing most people tend to recognize and appreciate even less. But it is this too. I refer not to that occasional death that ends years of intense suffering after which friends and relatives say, "It was a blessing." I mean that God planned well when he planned life with an end to it. That life has a limit is good—and it is no limitation.

An uncut diamond of any size can be made into a perfect jewel; that is to say, can be given meaning. The only limitation is the skill of the cutter. If the craftsman is master enough, perfection can be achieved in any size—any, that is, which is reasonably comprehensible to you and me. Here is what I mean when I say that death is a blessing. If life were endless, *that* would indeed be a limitation, an actual detracting factor in man's struggle to infuse his life with meaning. It would be hard, for example, to imagine a diamond cutter doing anything meaningful with a diamond the size, let us say, of Mount Washington. Of course there is something impressive about sheer size—even as there is about great age. But so far as meaning is concerned, as with a work of art (a drama that takes six hours to perform, for example), this tends to be a distracting factor.

Quality, perfection, beauty, meaning, pattern, direction, purpose—all are words that imply a framework, boundaries, a beginning and an end. For God it may be otherwise, but we are finite, and this is exactly what it means to be finite—to need death in order to give meaning to life. "The days of our age are threescore years and ten, and though men be strong that they come to fourscore years; yet is their strength then but labour and sorrow; so soon passeth it away, and we are gone." If we consider it tragic that some men have been cut off in the prime of life, as we say, then we ought to acknowledge that it is also tragic that others have lived on too far past their prime. The first problem is not senility but meaninglessness. To be in good physical health at the age of one hundred is rare, but not nearly so rare as still to be living a meaningful and productive life at the age of one hundred. It is a blessing that our bodies give out, thereby putting a more or less decent period at the end of our lives. It is hard enough, even so, to keep our existence filled with some significance. Death, therefore, is one of the great blessings of life.

When Jesus said, "It is finished.", I believe he said it not sadly. He said it more as an artist might say it, after having put the last touches on a painting, or as a poet might say it, after he had completed the last line of a sonnet. Death was welcomed, not as an end to suffering or relief from strain, but as the proper limit of life— its undeniable finality serving to remind you and me that we, even as Our Lord, have not all the time in the world. It serves also as a blessing, the blessing of numbered days, such as a man might hope to be able to handle in a way to please God.

In the annals of history there have been, among unbelievers, plenty of men who were brave in the face of death. And among believers, even among the most devout, there have been many whose faith has faltered. But the weight of evidence nevertheless is heavily in favor of those who believe. They best can appreciate the mystery, as mystery, without insisting that they understand. They manage somehow to preserve their dignity and their integrity, at the same time acknowledging that this mystery may be too high for them. So they can stand in reverence and awe but not fear, knowing death to be an instrument of God, and therefore to some purpose.

Marriage

Lots of people get married. Among those who never do, most would have liked to, and probably they have spent much time thinking about, and yearning for, the state of matrimony. And virtually everyone has had parents who were married and thereby had occasion early to observe the institution and form some theories about it. Like death, marriage is a fact of life with which most people have to deal in some context or other. Here too I say that I believe that people with faith are a little better armed than people without.

I would like to begin, however, with a discussion of the state of not being married, an aspect of marriage of paramount importance to many and one too blandly brushed aside by the married world. From holy writ and from the evidence of science and common sense, it is obvious that marriage is the proper, intended, practical, and desired condition of life for adult humans. For most people, therefore, to be unmarried is a misfortune. The married world, in its comfortable majority, is much too callous about this. It is so easy to gloss over the pain of others, to make excuses, and to confuse one's own simple good fortune with virtue. "She could have got married if she hadn't been so damned particular." "He doesn't need to get married. He's in love with his job." There is a quiet cruelty rampant among the married which is appalling. I call attention to it, not so much as admonition but to emphasize that the married state is normal and proper and ought to be made to work. The alternative, most often, is less good, and the test which it puts to one's faith enormous. Still, faith can make a difference, here as elsewhere.

What both the propensity to get married and the relative unhappiness of the unmarried bear witness to is the fact that no one can afford to live unto himself. Of course being married does not guarantee that one will not try, but for the unmarried a special effort to avoid it is required. The threats of uselessness and self-centeredness are just more severe, their flames fanned as they are by loneliness.

But faith, it seems to me, is well-designed to combat those very challenges. The question of religious celibacy comes first to mind, not because it is the answer for any but a very few in this world but because it brings certain issues into sharp focus. To marry the church has been proved by some to be a reasonable and successful and happy alternative to marrying a husband or a wife, even though sins have been committed in the name of this kind of marriage as in the other. Faith must be strong. Devotion may be intense. Self-discipline must be the order of every waking hour. But these aspects of faith have made a difference to lives so ordered, and that is the point I want to make here.

Marriage

Among devout religious celibates, uselessness and self-centeredness and loneliness have very often and very successfully been conquered—by faith. Not dispelled, but conquered!

Among most unmarried people, however, such a solution to the problem is obviously too extreme. Nevertheless, to the extent that one can bring faith to bear, the same kind of help is available and the same kind of victory possible. Both the unmarried woman who has been "too damned particular" and the unmarried man who "is in love with his job" bear witness to one truth—that marriage is not really the be-all and end-all of life, even though it may be the desirable and proper arrangement for people living together in pairs. To some extent at least, most unmarried people are unmarried by choice; that is, they have rejected the idea that they should accept any marriage just to be married. And to the same extent, they have achieved dignity and merit respect from the married world, some of whom have been less particular and less high-principled.

This does not mean that there is no suffering or that they are wholly satisfied with their lot. There may be as much anguish behind the scenes of the apparently serene permanent bachelor who seems to have solved all through his genuine love of his work as there is behind the scenes of some apparently idyllic marriages. The grass is not entirely green on either side of the fence, though, as always, it tends to seem greener on the far side. I have known two unmarried men in my life who seemed to me most successfully to have coped with the state of permanent bachelorhood. They both were men who professed and practiced an orthodox religious faith and, largely through it, I believe, achieved

a composure and a usefulness and love of life which
to the outward eye, at least, would seem to be one of
faith's first fruits. Of course the outward eye does not
see all. Who knows what pain and disappointment and
heartbreak may lie beneath such a smooth exterior?
Who indeed? But who knows how many of these same
evils may lie behind many a so-called perfect marriage?
In any case, effectiveness is something.

There are many unmarried people, however, who
might be willing to accept this thesis but who would
still cry out, "Well and good! So faith is the answer to
my plight. But it's not so easy. I have no such faith.
What am I supposed to do about that?" The question,
which is sure to beg itself at every turn, is fair and to
some extent unanswerable. I shall make some attempt
at an answer later, even though how to achieve faith is
not my central theme. Here I can only say that the cry
itself—the more desperate and the more indignant the
more convincing—does tend to bear witness to the
validity of the proposition that among the unmarried
people of this earth the believer has an edge.

It is time now to consider marriage. And the place
to begin is with the selection of a mate. There are two
theories. The romantic and the practical, they might
be called. According to the former, for each man there
is somewhere in this world one woman whom destiny
will introduce him to. And when they meet, they will
immediately recognize each other, because God intended it so. She will be referred to as "the" girl. According to the latter theory, it makes almost no difference
at all whom anyone marries. A bachelor friend of mine
told me one day that he had decided to get married.
Jokingly I said, "Do you have anyone in mind or is this

just a matter of principle?" Seriously he replied, "I have no one in mind. It is a matter of principle." Within a year he was married to a girl he had not met at the time of our conversation. Now, twenty years later, he is still married to her, and happily.

Any two people who have anything in common at all—and it needn't be much—who have any common decency and any desire to make a go of it can live happily, amicably, and even lovingly together for life. Though both theories of marriage are here purposely overstated, I tend to subscribe to the latter; only I would like to change the labels, for I think that this is truly the more romantic concept.

Consider how many ways husbands and wives can meet. I know a couple who met on a train going from Philadelphia to New York. They just struck up a conversation, followed up on the conversation, and eventually got married. Was this the hand of God? I do not think so. I call it pure chance. I know another exceptionally happily married couple whose romance started when at a New Year's Eve party his eye caught the lovely line of her figure "across a crowded room," one might say. I know another couple who were brought up together from early childhood as stepbrother and sister. She married someone else first and only after his death discovered in her stepbrother a magnificent husband. Medieval history has many accounts of matches made at court, without the consent of either husband- or wife-to-be. Some of these were terrible marriages and often there was a lot of cheating. But sometimes these arranged marriages were glorious. Marriages have been performed when both parties were little children, who were then taken back to their respective homes to be brought up expressly as the future mate of the other. Whatever the method of matchmaking, I strongly suspect that any random sampling of one versus another would show comparable statistics of success and failure, compatibility and incompatibility, grace and vulgarity.

What is important about the way the story starts is that nothing is important about the way the story starts. And the point needs to be made because all too often, when a marriage begins to fall apart, busybodies have a way of looking back at its beginning—as knowingly as Monday morning quarterbacks—saying, "Well, what could you expect?" I say, from the beginning one has a right to expect anything or nothing. What really matters is not the early circumstances but the people.

In my position as headmaster of a boys' school, it is my job every summer to match about fifty new boys, more or less blind, as room-mates. My batting average —without benefit of either sex or romance—is about as good as the marriage and divorce rate in the United States. The determining factor in both cases is not how well-matched people are but how decent, gracious, unselfish, and considerate they are. Naturally, under these circumstances, I believe that people whose lives are touched with religious faith make better husbands and wives than others, because I believe that such people tend, particularly under stress, to be more decent, gracious, unselfish, and considerate. Among the fruits of faith are the conquest of self, spiritual sensitivity, and plain, ordinary, common or garden morality. It is hard to see how these can fail to have a bearing on the success of any marriage.

Again, I do not say that these qualities automatically

exist in sufficient quantity and quality among all who appear to be people of faith or that they are wholly lacking among people who make no formal proclamation of faith. But the evidence is strong in favor of the faithful. And, more often than not, when it seems that the faith has not worked well, it is only because the world has misread the label. (A man cannot be considered a believer—in the sense in which I write—merely on the basis of his own say-so any more than he can be considered an unbeliever by the same evidence. But ask any hundred people, selected at random, to separate any other hundred people, also selected at random, into the faithful and the non-believers. Throw out all about whom there is any serious disagreement and, as in political pools, label them "undecided." Then compare the two groups that are left. See if those who have been recognized as religious people and believers—see if indeed they do not handle the problems of marriage better than the others. No one is in a position to be objective, surely not I. But from my subjective position I say the evidence of the efficacy of faith in marriage is overwhelming.)

Let us now consider some specific problems. The first might be put in the form of a question. In marriage, do two really become one? To what extent can or should or does a husband lose himself, his identity, his separateness in the new combined personage which is the couple? Somewhat of course. As there is cooperation, teamwork, mutual consideration, and self-sacrifice, a third entity is born out of what were two wholly separate entities. But is this team now sacred to the extent of completely obliterating the two separate entities that once existed? I think not. I think everyone thinks not,

when it is put to them so. But I also think that a great
many people so emphasize the sacredness of this new
third entity—particularly when talking about the marriage of someone else, or when chastising their own
mate—that as a practical, day-by-day consideration the
sacredness of the separateness is largely lost.

Common among young lovers is the notion that it is
the very height of romance to have no secrets from each
other. But how much more romantic it is to acknowledge that of course they must and should have secrets
from each other, and to respect the secrets of the other.
To try to deny the right of one's mate to an inviolable
inward self is to try to destroy an integral part of his
individuality and his humanity.

In spite of the references in holy writ and in the
various marriage services to two becoming one, that
idea is much more pagan than truly religious. It is
surely not Christian. In most Christian marriage services, the point is emphasized that *each* of *two* people
is coming forward to offer himself—as he is and will be
—to the other as a mate. They pledge separately. They
act, each on his own, making individual promises, one
giving and the other receiving a ring. They join hands,
not to make one hand, but two hands together—but still
and always two hands. Having been joined together
by God, they are to be put asunder by no man—only by
death. But they are not to be lost in each other. They
are to be found in each other—*each* found.

Neither Christianity nor any other formal religion
has a corner on this idea. But I do feel that among believers it is handled most successfully. It is an extremely
delicate notion, for the two *do* have to become one in
some sense and to some degree. The oneness *is* sacred;

it is only that it must not be so overwhelmingly sacred that the sacredness of separateness becomes desecrated. The balance is not only delicate, it is paradoxical. And only through faith can most paradoxes be found acceptable. A man who has learned through his faith to accept that most difficult idea of the Trinity, for example, is perhaps a little bit better armed for this aspect of marriage than one who has never even attempted such a venture of faith.

The importance to any marriage of the idea of two people being separate and one at the same time should hardly need emphasizing. If this idea is valid, as I believe it is, then it is vital. But what is most important from a practical standpoint is for a husband or a wife to know where he ought to be standing and which way he ought to be looking. Together they can easily—in theory at least—revere the sacredness of their oneness. What is difficult is for each to revere the sacredness of separateness—that is the *other's* separateness. The individuality with which each must be concerned is the individuality of the other. That looks simple on paper too. But how difficult it is for any married person to make this his or her first concern day by day. It takes patience and courage and self-discipline and self-sacrifice beyond anything anyone who has never tried it can possibly imagine. How easy it is to lose sight of the whole main point and to fight for one's *own* individuality at the expense of that of one's mate. It is pretty hard for any believer to see how the right path can be trod without the help of God—help not merely hoped for but constantly besought. The issue is the sin of pride, staggering enough for anyone on earth to cope with, but always devastating to those who do not even acknowledge that there is any such thing.

Marriage

The next problem is allied to the first; put indelicately but somewhat traditionally, it too consists of a question. Who wears the pants in the family? On the slim chance that some may never have heard it, I here repeat the proverbial story of the couple who had been absolutely happily married for twenty-five years. When asked to explain the secret of their success, the wife said, "It was easy. As soon as we were married, we agreed that all major decisions should be made by my husband and all minor decisions by me." On further questioning it turned out that so far, in twenty-five years, there had been no major decisions. This, of course, is one way to solve the problem. And in fact there just are not very many other ways. Anyone who has belonged to an organization of any size, from two up, knows that final responsibility for certain types of decisions must at last rest with one person. So to some extent either husband or wife must at last be the boss.

There are a million easy decisions that can be reached by mutual agreement arrived at through love or argument or both. Others are achieved by reason, or on the basis of a stronger *interest* on the part of one or the other in the issue. Nor should this fact be overlooked: too often it is *not* the tough and important decisions which cause the fights. Frequently the issue is not a right answer but simply a test of will. Theoretically, of course, love should bridge all such gorges, but sometimes it doesn't. When it fails, what is needed is a special, secret kind of self-discipline, a subjugation of the self so that a bruise to it seems less important than the preservation of harmony.

Such self-discipline and self-subjugation are not easy, for there are few things about which humans tend to be more selfish than ideas. And, if you think you are

right, you are awfully tempted to feel that proving it
is a kind of crusade, all in the name of Truth—instead
of merely ego-flexing, which, in fact, it often really is.

My father, who was really happily married only after
three tries, learned this basic truth with difficulty and
at a high price, but he learned it at last more nobly
than any man I ever knew. It was not a question of
subservience or sentimental wife-worship or lack of
self-confidence. He was just able to see that sometimes
(not always, but most of the time) harmony is the most
important issue of the moment. To know that much and
to be able to act upon it a man needs both the perspective and the power of his faith.

For a wife (or a husband) to make all the minor
decisions is not such a bad arrangement. And for a
couple to have faced no major decisions in twenty-five
years is not entirely fantastic. Of course it is a *little*
fantastic. But not nearly so much so as that there should
be as *many* major decisions as the number of battles
in most marriages would seem to indicate. Harmony is
important. Fights are important too, but the notion that
they are wholly and lightly justified by the fun of making up is a dangerous exaggeration which does not
sufficiently take into account the harm that has been
done. I am not speaking now of scars, the bitter wounds
of heated words. Few of these are permanent, and even
the permanent ones are not always bad. I am speaking
rather of the waste of precious life. An hour or a day
or a month spent in fighting is spent out of who knows
how little store? And it is gone—and with it some life.
To keep peace in the family is to keep peace. Not very
many issues are more important.

Still, there are major decisions, truly major. Generally they have to do with bringing up children or a man's (or his wife's) career. Who decides? And who decides who decides? Must this always be a test of strength? I believe that it can as well be a test of faith, and through it love. Grace, faith's favorite daughter, here stands in the sun, reflecting her rays so brightly as to dispel many a shadow. Nowhere, perhaps, does the need for separateness impress itself more. For two people have to decide, not together but separately. The question is again, as with minor decisions, one of will, of pride, of self. Only now the issue is more delicate. Perhaps now harmony, for a time, cannot be of first importance. Just how hard do you fight? Maybe this time you really *are* crusading in the name of Truth. Maybe you really *do* know better. Maybe you really are *required* to save your mate from herself by forcing your decision upon her. But how can you be sure? By faith only. And then only by faith, which is to say you *cannot* be *sure*. The decision must at last be yours alone. God help you! Ask Him, and He will.

A third specific problem in marriage is suggested by the word *balance*. Can the rewards and duties, the inner turmoil and inner calm, be kept in balance? The extremely obvious answer is that they cannot. But it is nevertheless astonishing how often an unhappy husband or wife blames unhappiness on some inequality in a particular situation, or perhaps in the entire relationship. "It is not fair!" is the common cry. One of the problems of marriage, then, is that IT IS NOT FAIR ... ever.

The situation is complicated by the elusive subtlety of the word "fair." What is fair? In a permanent relationship between two people, with the infinite complexities of each, the ever changing moods and psyches and situations, truly, honestly and literally—only God knows. The question is too difficult and too subjective for anyone else to be able to arrive anywhere near the truth. More important, who ever said it would or could be fair? On this score the original, romantic protestations of love are generally more enlightened than many feelings and ideas which often replace them in later years. Personalities *cannot* be neatly balanced. Circumstances make demands on one that are not made on the other—illness, the pressure of a work assignment, pregnancy, failure to receive a hoped-for promotion, menopause, to mention only a few of the predictable ones. It has often been said that in any marriage one partner is always the essential giver and the other the taker. Probably this is so, but seldom do the roles remain permanently the same. They change. And each time they change there is need for adjustment. After all, it *is* more blessed to give than to receive (though too often in our stubborn pride we insist otherwise). And to change back and forth from the more to the less blessed, and to know which is which, tries the soul.

Most Christian marriage services have in essence this thought: "for better for worse, for richer for poorer, in sickness and in health, to love and to cherish, till death us do part." The light-hearted, eager, starry-eyed enthusiasm with which most brides and grooms utter these words quite blind them to the sober nature of the pledge. It is very specific and very inclusive and very clear. Yet the cry, "It is not fair!", often so soon uttered, is a first beginning of a renunciation. To be sure, there are times when the "worse" or the "poorer" or the "sickness" go so far beyond what anyone might reasonably have expected that sympathy, deep sympathy, is needed and deserved. More often, however, the disappointment or the falling short or the misfortune do, indeed, lie within the bounds of reasonable expectation. Life is less idyllic than it seems to young lovers, but, however exalted their love, they cannot hide from life's realities. The absolutely inescapable imbalance in the relationship of any husband and wife will always try their love. If there is no faith by which that love may be bolstered, then the marriage may move relentlessly toward the breaking point. Only if love is supported by faith, I believe, can it reach its highest beauty. It is not in balance but out of balance that love shines most gloriously.

Now it is time to turn to the nature of the marriage bond, where, it seems to me, the role of faith is clarified. A religious marriage service is predicated on the belief that God is present, not just as a witness but as a participant. It is to Him directly that vows are made, by Him bound. It is true that the groom, taking his bride's hand and facing her, says, "I, James, take thee Joan, to my wedded wife." But prior to that, facing the priest or clergyman, he has already answered a direct question. "Wilt thou have this woman to thy wedded wife, to live together after God's ordinance in the holy estate of matrimony?" And he has said, not to his bride but directly to the man of God, "I will." That is an unconditional pledge to which he willingly binds himself and is bound. Because it is made to God, it is sacred. At the time he may not know what he is saying and doing, but through faith, during the succeeding twenty or fifty years, he will discover.

I believe that marriage is not a contract but a religious act. The difference is crucial and the implications endless. In essence a contract says, "If you do so and so, I will do so and so." The implication obviously is that, if you do not, neither need I. It takes two parties to make a contract valid. But one person can make a vow and without any ifs be held to it by his own morality and the help of God. This is the very essence of the separateness—even loneliness?—of getting married. For the believer, this fact of a third person present and participating is the source of all future patience, strength, and perspective about himself. Exactly to the extent that he truly believed in the holy nature of what he did (or came to believe in its holiness) will his marriage be successful. Surely, it is better to believe.

What about divorce? From what I have written my answer must be fairly obvious. But lest I seem to pontificate about this delicate subject, let me say first that my mother and father were divorced; my aunt and uncle were divorced; my grandfather and grandmother were divorced; and a fairly large number of other people whom I love have been divorced. On a few rare occasions I have advised people to get divorced. Still I think divorce is never justified, seldom the right answer. It is pretty hard to argue persuasively in favor of breaking a bond which one considers to be sacred, to put asunder what one believes God to have joined together. Certainly cheap divorces are cheap, and most divorces are cheap. They are predicated on the theory that some things (like happiness) are more important than they really are; that some things (like infidelity) are more unforgivable than they really are; that some things (like compatability) are more essential than they really are. They are also often predicated on a dreamy conception of what a marriage *ought* to be like, on childish

Marriage

notions which utterly fail to take human nature into account.

What, then, are justifiable grounds for divorce? None is *justifiable*. How can anyone, under any circumstances, *justify* breaking a vow? Divorce, in the eyes of a merciful God, might, it seems to me, be *forgiven* when the marriage has become unbearable. And then the forgiveness would have to be sought, begged for, on one's knees, from God alone. When is the marriage unbearable? That each man must decide for himself, tutored by his conscience as well as strengthened, hopefully, by his faith.

In selecting marriage as a paramount illustration of the efficacy of faith, I have inevitably implied that making any marriage work is a tough proposition. What I have said might lead a few to suppose that I have a rather cynical, unromantic attitude toward it. I believe I have not. I do think, however, that even with romance and sex and mature love and children to help things along, it is not easy for any two people to live a lifetime together. It is a major challenge to one's faith and a major proving ground for its efficacy. Romance and love and joy are facts—indeed I believe they are gifts of God. They are like a trousseau, freely given by a loving father to clothe a bride . . . but not for life. Eventually she must, with her husband's help, buy her own clothes, as well as mend and alter and clean them. Those who complain that their youthful romance has slipped away with their youth are as foolish and irresponsible as if they were to expect to be clothed forever from a trousseau. The romance of later years—like the clothes on one's back—must be earned, by faith, I believe. It is not less romantic for that, but more, for it is

Marriage

of difficulty and disagreement and suffering that this later romance is built, not of selfish, lazy, saccharine sentimentality.

On the subject of marriage, St. Paul, a single man, said, "I say therefore to the unmarried and widows, it is good for them if they abide even as I. But if they cannot contain, let them marry: for it is better to marry than to burn." On the basis of this meager accolade, he is cited as an authority in the marriage service itself, which, speaking of the holy estate of matrimony, says ,"and is commended of St. Paul to be honorable among all men." Some commendation. Mae West is said to have put it more succinctly. "Marriage is a great institution. But who needs an institution?" It seems that most of the world does, and whatever the trials and tribulations, most people make it work pretty well. St. Paul and Mae West to the contrary notwithstanding, I believe that the institution was ordained of God. After his creation, Adam was kept pretty busy for a while thinking up names for animals and birds and things. But his tasks didn't provide companionship and there is sadness in the line, "but for Adam there was not found an help meet for him." So Eve was created. "Therefore shall a man leave his father and his mother, and shall cleave unto his wife." To be able to believe this, as a word of God, is to be better married than not to be able to believe it.

Children

This chapter is purposely misnamed. It is, you will soon see, not about children at all. It is about parents. But all parents at least pretend to be interested in children and in what is written about children, hoping, presumably from what they read, to learn something about other people's children that will make them feel better about their own. Urged on by this hope, they are willing, even eager, to read almost anything about children. But when they are confronted by a printed page about parents, they shy away. Nobody really likes to be criticized and most parents are firmly on their guard. They would rather not listen than be told. So let the title stand as is. But let all readers be warned that most of what will be said here about children is intended primarily to serve as a mirror, in which parents may see themselves.

In the adult world there are two classic expressions of attitudes toward children: one may be symbolized by the sentimental phrase "pitter patter of little feet" and the other by the rude word "brats." Both are exaggerations and misrepresentations. Yet each does suggest something of the genuine feelings that adults have about children. It is a pity (but an understandable pity) that the "pitter patter" attitude is most common among those who do not have children or do not have much to do with children. The "brat" attitude is most common among those who do. Both are understandable because it just happens to be true that, no matter how much one loves children—his own or anyone else's—they are a burden and a trial as well as a mystery to the adult world. Vice versa too (but that is another matter). So, once again, faith becomes a critical factor. Anyone who is going to bring up children needs help—and faith is the best help he can get.

Let us begin at the beginning—with fatherhood, since the author is a father. Motherhood is different, but not as completely different as is sometimes supposed. The beginning is the waiting room of the maternity wing of a hospital. Too many books and movies and cartoons have depicted the scene to make it worth describing again in any detail. There is anxiety. There are also dreams. These have to do first of all with the sex. Will it be a girl or a boy? Some fathers pretend they do not care, and others are very frank and open. The first are generally liars. The second are selfish, presumptuous, and sacrilegious fellows who hope to excuse and cover all with candor. Fortunately, however, in neither case does it make much difference, since the sex of a child is one thing about a child which parents so far have not found a way to control. The day will come when science will change all that, but let us meanwhile rejoice that that day is not quite yet. It is good to think that God

still has something to say about what your child is
destined to be like.

Even while this question is still unsettled, the ex-
pectant father has other things to dream about. And
what glorious dreams they are. Such unbelievable detail! If it is to be a daughter: her beauty, the color of
her eyes and hair, her education, her social life, those
delightful little times alone with her father, the boy-
friends of the future and their formal presentation to
father for his approval or disapproval. Or if it is to be a
son: his handsomeness (not so much detail needed here,
just the spitting image of his father), his athletic prow-
ess (achieved through hundreds of hours of practice
with his father), his education (can't apply for admission to father's college at birth any more, but you can
still dream), and then a distinguished career (either in
father's business or one of the more dignified profes-
sions). A lifetime here, in a few hours.

Then the doctor appears with a reassuring smile and
announces the sex. Boy or girl. That was the only miss-
ing punch in the IBM card, so that, as soon as it is sup-
plied, out pops the card, complete. In retrospect, the
father will be amazed that he could have had such an
involved picture all ready for himself. It was like un-
furling a flag—one shake and it is flying in the breeze,
with every star and every stripe glistening in the sun.

The world looks with indulgent good humor on this
familiar scene. It all seems so pleasantly innocent
enough and harmless. Innocent it surely is, but I am
not sure it is harmless. The fact is that such a father
has just committed the cardinal sin of pride. He has
confused himself with God. He has planned a life—not
his own—but one very likely shaped after his own

Children

image. Nor is that dream often easily set aside. Sometimes, tragically, it becomes a controlling force for years to come. It will not be very long before the father will be going back to dear old Princeton for his fifth reunion, taking his three-year-old son with him and buying him a T-shirt with "Class of 19?" on the front, thinking that it is still all in good fun. It is not fun. It is a sin, and potentially at least, a terrible sin. He is being possessive about another human being—a small human being, who just happens to be his son. The father will spend a good many years trying to teach his son to respect him, but already he does not respect his son. At least he does not respect the most important thing about him—that his son is somebody else. Thereby the father is sowing seeds of all kinds of mischief for the future. If his son turns out well, pleasing to his father and in accordance with that old dream (revised to be sure), then his father is going to take inordinate pride in him. If the boy turns out badly (not in conformity to the dream), then father—incongruously and unfairly—is going to hold his son to blame. Had he, in that hospital waiting room prayed to God Almighty, thanking Him first for the miracle of a new life brought into the world, then asking His blessing and His direction for that new life, and humbly asking for some guidance as a father—so that he might serve first neither his son nor himself but God—that start would have gone far to avoid the future mischief, not to say the agony for all.

I know a couple who were married for ten years before they had a child. Then at last a daughter was born, whom they proceeded to spoil so shockingly that their friends at last found courage enough to object. The child's mother was not disturbed. She was confident.

Children

"I waited ten years for my child," she said, "and if I want to spoil her nobody is going to stop me." Nobody has stopped her and the trouble has begun. The question arises, is your child yours?

To the believer the answer is NO, and that answer makes a difference. I believe that in the eyes of God the parents are charged with heavy responsibilities toward and for their children—but *no* rights. What God has in mind for our children is what shall be—if parents do not too wilfully foul up the works—and usually that is good news for the child. One of the quickest ways to find out that God is smarter than we are is to try to usurp His right to make our children into what He intends them to be and see what happens. Even among the so-called heathen it is traditional to stand in awe and wonder at what God has wrought, for the first few days of a baby's life. "Look at the little hands and little feet, so perfect and complete!" To the extent that such awe and wonder can continue, parenthood is blessed and bearable. Too often it is cursed just to the extent that parents take over as though there were no God.

There are two kinds of parents. One rolls up his sleeves and sets about moulding a life, if not after his own image at least after his image of his image. Because God did not intend it so, this turns out to be hard work, excruciatingly painful for parent and child alike. Too often the trouble is that without consulting God parents assume that what they must create is a silk purse. And, sadly, if the material is unsuited the results will be tragic. Of a certain creature whose future was for a time uncertain but eventually determined, Alice in Wonderland said, "If it had grown up it would have made a dreadfully ugly child; but it makes a rather handsome pig, I think."

On the other hand, that parent who can continue the wonder of those first days, remembering the "what God hath wrought" part, and taking no particular credit for what transpires, nor overly constrained to fix blame when there is temptation to blame, will be thankful for what seems good and will find the courage and patience to accept what seems bad or incomprehensible to him, always confident that God knows what He is doing.

One can imagine with what consternation the parents of Helen Keller must have accepted the fate of their child from the hands of God, so shockingly different from the dreams they must have had. But when, with our limited human knowledge, bolstered by hindsight, we consider this whole story and its significance to so many—its intimate human relationship, as well as its impact on the whole world—would anyone say that God did not know what He was doing? He does not promise that every child will grow up as its parents wish, or even as God wishes. Nor does He promise that there will be no such thing as pain or disappointment or genuine tragedy. He promises only that somehow all things will "work together for good to them that love God."

There are few things for which we ought to be more grateful to God than the fact that His ways are not our ways, that our wishes do not more often come true— most particularly as far as our children are concerned.

Is the parents' job therefore simply to stand aside and contemplate their child with wonder and gratitude and courage and faith? Certainly not—though this extreme

Children

is not likely to be any *more* ruinous than its opposite. As I have said, parents do have responsibilities. They must feed and clothe and teach their children. In general this is obvious, though about the teaching—that is, what and how much and with what passion—very little is obvious. However piously a parent may teach in the name of God, with every lesson he runs the risk of presumption; and the surer he is that the ground on which he stands is pure and holy, the more he must beware. For it is just in the name of all that's holy that the worst sins are committed.

What most parents do (and I include myself, since twenty years of teaching other people's children has taught me nothing about how to bring up my own) is to admit that all that I have said, psychologically and morally (and perhaps religiously) is sound. They say, "Of course I want my child to grow up to be whatever he is destined to be. There are just one or two things I insist upon!" A father once said to me, "There are only two things I want from my son, that he stop biting his nails and that he get a decent haircut. I told him that if he'd do that, I'd buy him a new Cadillac Eldorado for his graduation. Now, isn't that fair?"

Believe me. The story is true though it may seem impossibly silly. It is remarkable only in its largesse. The nails and the haircut are not unusual issues of contention. (Since the above incident took place, I have come to dispute with one of my own sons on exactly those issues.) What is really at issue is separate wills. The irate father chose to make an issue of these particular items—though the boy in question had a lot of other faults that were worse. What the father did not realize was that his son had chosen these items first, to make the issue. "Then what am I supposed to do?" cries a frustrated father. Speaking as a headmaster and a clergyman and a father, I do not know. I just do not know. But the purpose of the story is to illustrate that the problem of what to teach one's child, the question of how far to go, is not an easy one. It will try a man's or a woman's soul for fair! The price of teaching some lessons, however important they may seem to parents, eventually becomes just too high.

For the man or woman with the love of God in his or her heart, and not merely the love of self and the love of child, the issues can be settled with a little more confidence and the outcome more graciously accepted. Such faith in God invariably reflects itself in greater faith in one's child. Such faith enables a parent to contemplate failure—his child's failure as well as his own—without undue consternation, as part of life, as something that can be overcome, out of which much good may emerge. Such faith may even bolster that old-fashioned notion that the best way to bring up a child to be the kind of person he ought to be is for parents to arrange their own lives so that they are the kind of people *they* ought to be. Such faith brings a mother and a father to church every Sunday, where they confess their sins, perhaps kneeling shoulder to shoulder with a daughter or a son, reminded at least once a week that God is God, and nobody else.

I do not mean to imply that there are no issues on which parents should hold ground, or that one easily or often arrives at the conclusion that for the teaching of this or that lesson the price is too high. No adult can in conscience often decide that the greatest good is being served by succumbing to the will of a child. But it *can* happen, and a wisdom tutored by faith is most likely to know when it should. "I can of my own self do nothing: as I hear, I judge: and my judgment is just; because I seek not mine own will, but the will of the Father which hath sent me." The words are from Jesus and no mere mortal could presume to utter them with His confidence. Still they suggest a spirit which I think most parents, as parents, would find it hard to improve upon.

Among the casually committed there is a graph of reverence for "what God hath wrought" in children which can be plotted with fair consistency. As I have said, there are few who are not moved at least to think of God, if not to thank Him, for the miracle of birth and new life. Birth, like death, is a moment which deeply moves the hearts of most, and a heart so moved is touched with at least some kind of faith. It is humbled, which is nothing more than proper perspective, one of faith's gifts. For quite some time thereafter, the gratitude continues, not yet too badly marred by pride. A little child saying his prayers, or asleep sucking his fingers contentedly, or playing with the soap in the bath, or taking his first step, or uttering his first word, still has the power to suggest the eternal to most hearts, whether tutored in the church or not. "Of such," said Jesus, "is the Kingdom of heaven:" and we believe Him. This is innocence. And innocence is as beautiful as a sunset, with the same power to fill hearts with the goodness of life—a hint of the goodness of God.

With the passage of time, however, the innocence wears off. Gratitude and wonder give way to suspicion and anxiety, which may express themselves in terms of anger and wilfulness (the parents'), until at length God is forgotten altogether and the devil takes over. One must assume that there was not much innocence left in the faces of the children who were said once so to have gawked at W.C. Fields that he turned and said to them, "Back to Reform School, nose-pickers!" The remark is famous because too many in the adult world have said in their hearts, "You tell 'em, W.C.!" It really is hard not to be sympathetic with Mr. Fields, for as children grow up they are an expanding trial. They strain nearly every decent instinct a grown person may have. They can be cruel, heartless, ungrateful, thoughtless, crude, stubborn, and very nearly unlovable. "Little children step on your feet; big children on your heart." runs an ancient proverb of Provence.

The faithful are certainly not exempt from the tortures suffered by other parents. But, from my fairly intimate association with some twelve hundred sets of parents and children, it seems to me that the believers come out a little better and so do their children. As I have already suggested more than once, this is not a scientific study, nor am I trying to lead anyone down the path of logic to the truth of faith. I am recording in a most subjective way my own observations. From my own experience I can say that there is nothing in all the world that I am surer of than that religious people make better parents than non-religious people. (I mean that word "religious" to exclude hypocrites—which by definition it does.) Indeed faith is so generally recognized to be efficacious in the realm of bringing up children that some parents adopt the outward and visible signs for the express purpose—and only for that purpose—of bringing up their children. Of course the pretense doesn't work because it is not genuine. But it

does bear witness to the fact that such people realize
that faith has some relevance in this important aspect
of life.

Until now I have used the word children to discuss
offspring of every age from a new-born baby to an
adolescent. Naturally generalizations about so varied a
group of people with such divergent problems are
bound to miss the mark a good deal of the time. Let us,
therefore, be more specific, choosing one area generally
considered difficult—adolescence. I choose this area not
wholly arbitrarily. My first and best reason is that I
have spent my whole life in the secondary school world
and therefore perhaps know more about adolescence
than about other aspects of childhood. What is more
important, I think that it is in just this area, where the
problems are so many and so complex, that faith—on
the part of parents—is most helpful and most needed.

I know that in suggesting this I fly in the face of most
of the best learning of the best of child psychologists,
most of whom speak of the formative years as being
earlier than adolescence. Some people attribute to the
Roman Catholic Church the notion that, if they can
have a child up to the age of seven, he will in the long
run be theirs. There is no denying the importance of
the early years; surely they are sometimes decisive. But
it does seem to me that to a large extent instinct serves
parents and children as well or better than elaborate
theory, in those early years. Faith is more natural. It
can be less conscious. In her child's infancy, a human
mother, like a mother robin, knows pretty much what
to do under most circumstances. What is peculiar to
humans is that their function as parents lasts so much
longer than the parenthood of animals and birds. And

so it is for the long pull that they must resort to their human qualities—specifically human—to see them through. One of these is faith, and I am very much persuaded that there is a crescendo of need for it which follows the calendar of birthdays very closely.

In launching into the subject of adolescence, I realize that I run the risk of losing readers. So much has been written on the subject that, however interested one may be, his first reaction is likely to be a groan and a deaf ear; or, to quote my daughter at the age of five, "Not again!" I can only plead that what I have to say is not academic, that I have no easy formula for the handling of adolescents and that I absolutely despise the word adolescent itself. Furthermore, I do not consider myself in any position to preach on the subject. All I want to do here is to try to describe what an adolescent is, and I confess I approach even that limited goal with fear. My qualifications are simply that I have seen a lot of these people, and I once was an adolescent myself.

According to an ancient Hebrew legend, to be able to identify the spirit is to be able to have some influence on it. Some years ago at Wooster School, where I have spent most of my adult life teaching, we had a senior prom week end and emptied the boys out of one of the dormitories and turned it over to the girls who were spending the night. Naturally strict instructions were given to the boys to stay completely away from that building. Long after the dance was over and the lights were out, my wife, a chaperone, heard a prowler outside and called for help. One of the masters responded, and as he came toward the building, saw a boy skirting the lawn. He called out to the boy to stop. Of course the boy did not. Then suddenly, miraculously, in a flash of moonlight he recognized the boy and called him by name. "Moore!" he said. "Moore!" And the boy promptly tripped and fell flat on his face in the driveway. It *was* Moore.

Perhaps, whatever our goal, if we could only have some reasonable idea of who an adolescent is, without even trying to go any further, we could better help him —and ourselves as well.

What is an adolescent? According to one school of thought, he is half animal and half human. This brings to mind a centaur. About a centaur one encyclopedia has this to say:

> Centaurs are often represented drawing the car of Dionysius, or bound and ridden by Eros, an illusion to their drunken and amorous habits. Their general character is that of wild, lawless and inhospitable beings, the slaves of their animal passions. . . . They are variously explained by a fancied resemblance to the shapes of clouds, or as spirits of the rushing mountain torrents or winds. Perhaps the likeliest suggestion is that they are a distorted recollection of some savage tribe. . . . Like the defeat of the Titans by Zeus, the contests with the centaurs typified the struggle between civilization and barbarism.

Everything said about a centaur is not applicable to adolescents, but some similarities are striking, including the use of Dionysius' car!

"Bound and ridden by Eros." Let us not pretend that this is not so. One does not need to get very deeply involved in the psychology of Freud to recognize that Eros does indeed bind and ride and that to the young colt or filly Eros is a strange and terrifying rider. Perhaps in our day we are so overcome by the apparent sophistication of the young that we are blinded to the fact that there is still much fear and great confusion. When I was a boy, venereal diseases and the likely possibilities of pregnancy kept a lot of people chaste. Now, thanks to modern science—adult science—the fears of my childhood are no longer effective restraints. On the whole that is a good thing, too, since as moral weapons they were immoral.

So hard does Eros ride that I have found that almost no line of talk is very effective, either in practice *or in theory*. The hundreds of boys with whom I have talked are not only not deterred, they are not even persuaded. Their honesty, I must say, is winsome. Morality, which they take to be custom—and is it not?—does not move them. There is a flicker of light only when God is mentioned. Strangely enough, they do know what sin is. And they do see its pertinence.

"Slaves of their animal passions"—not Eros only but other passions as well. Consider food! Have you ever seen a teen-age boy eat? There is testimony to support the fact that when I was that age I ate that way myself, but even so I cannot now believe my eyes. They say that it is different with girls, but I am not even so sure of that. When nobody is looking, my daughter can stack it away with the best of her three brothers. But it is not the quantity that is impressive; it is the *passion*. How do they *breathe?* I ask myself. The answer, I suppose, is that they breathe food. A number of years ago at Wooster, a young man named Sullivan was elected captain of the football team. The announcement was made in the dining room amid cheers and cries of, "Speech! Speech!" Young Mr. Sullivan stood up, waved his hand for silence—with a bit of an Irish flair—and, when it was achieved, said, "Pass the pudadas!" Eros, Hunger—and Fear. Fear of being alone, fear of being together, fear of being the same, fear of being different, fear of failure, and equally, fear of success. And along with fear, hate—hate of others and hate of self. And along with hate, love—love of others and love of self. "Slaves of their animal passions."

"Spirits of the rushing mountain torrents." Clear, splashing, fresh water, cascading uncontrollably down from the mysterious, beautiful, snow-capped mountain top of childhood's magnificent innocence, never to return, but hopefully to irrigate anew the valley below which the adult world calls civilization.

"Civilization and barbarism." Of course there is a war. Some adolescents are beat (though that word will be long out-of-date before this book goes to press). Some are "dead-end kids" (a durable phrase and problem). And some actually are criminals. Others are just unpleasant—"inhospitable," to quote the encyclopedia again. The centaur is half man and half horse. But when you meet a centaur, it is relatively easy to tell which end is which. With some adolescents, the distinctions are not always so obvious.

There is a war. What is not so clear is who is responsible for it. "Perhaps the likeliest suggestion is that (the centaurs) are a distorted recollection of some savage tribe." Could that savage tribe be you and me?

That brings up the question of the parenthood of centaurs. Their mother was named Nephele. She was famous for having tried to rescue her son from sacrifice to Zeus. It seems that this particular mother did the right thing. But rescuing their young is something mothers of adolescents can easily overdo, especially when those young get near the upper regions of adolescence. The centaurs' father was a fellow named Ixion, who, because of an extra-curricular love affair, was consigned forever to "infernal regions," where he was strapped to a huge wheel that went round and round forever. The infernal regions might have been Madison Avenue or Wall Street. And the wheel might have been the commuter's train, though there seems to be real doubt about the latter's going round and round forever. In any case, some adolescents share with the centaurs the fate of having a preoccupied father.

There is one more thing to say about centaurs. It was magnificently illustrated by a cartoon which appeared some years ago in a national magazine. It showed a mother centaur and a father centaur standing together, their arms folded over their chests, watching their young son gamboling in the fields. The caption was, "Don't you think it is about time we told him he's a myth?" I suppose the word adolescent has some semantic function, though, as I have suggested earlier, I have always hated it. But I am sure that through the years it has accrued to itself a vast amount of myth, so much so that it is probably a healthy thing for all of us to ask ourselves now and then whether or not there really is any such thing. If there were no such word, we might be forced to call these creatures fellow humans.

I ask you now to turn from a Greek myth to a Roman philosopher, from the centaur to Marcus Aurelius, from criticism to high praise. When I was an adolescent, I kept a little notebook of quotations which, for one reason or another, impressed me. Very recently I came upon that notebook some thirty years after I first started writing in it. One quotation from Marcus Aurelius particularly struck me. "Keep true to the dreams of thy youth."

Why should Marcus Aurelius have said such a thing? Clearly because the dreams of youth are better dreams than those of later years and because it is not easy—perhaps it is even impossible—as the years pass to keep to such dreams. This is an aspect of the adolescent which is more wonderful than anything he can ever achieve later on. It is as far removed from centaurs as night from day. If there is a war going on between civilization and barbarism, there are times in that war when it is we who are on the side of barbarism and our sons and daughters who are on the side of civilization. We speak often of the things they do and say which we find shocking. It seldom occurs to us that they too can be shocked by the things we do and say.

The idealism of youth is the purest idealism in all the world. Age often adds more dullness than wisdom. Vachel Lindsay's *The Leaden-Eyed* says as much very movingly. It is a sad poem, accusing the world, the adult world, of the great crime of destroying youth's dreams.

Let not young souls be smothered out before
They do quaint deeds and fully flaunt their pride.
It is the world's one crime its babes grow dull,
Its poor are ox-like, limp and leaden-eyed.
Not that they starve, but starve so dreamlessly,
Not that they sow, but that they seldom reap,
Not that they serve, but have no gods to serve,
Not that they die, but that they die like sheep.

Children

One Saturday afternoon in the spring I wandered into our school chapel balcony just after lunch. I looked down and saw a single boy in a back pew, on his knees in prayer. He did not see me. After a bit he got up, and on his way out picked up his tennis racket. It dawned suddenly upon me that he, the captain of the tennis team, was about to play an important match. Clearly he had been praying for victory. But that morning in Bible class he had argued with me about the existence of God. Since he was an adolescent, there was no reason why his argument that there is no God should keep him from praying to God. It was, in Vachel Lindsay's words, a "quaint deed" but also glorious, more glorious than most of the adult world is capable of.

Adolescents can sometimes be very confused about different loyalties. But loyalty is something they understand better than most of the rest of the world. The boy or girl who in a given instance allows his or her loyalty to a friend to supersede parental loyalty is sometimes chastised by the parents for not knowing what loyalty is all about. But generally the accusation is off the mark. At worst the child has been unable to handle an assignment in the conflict of loyalties, though even that is sometimes questionable. Indeed, most of the time I am inclined to think that the concept of loyalty is very well understood.

A few years ago a boy at Wooster had to be asked to leave the school. He was in real trouble. He had stolen quite a lot of money from a fairly large number of boys. He had also stolen personal belongings. Finally he stole a car. After he had gone, a friend of his who had roomed with him the year before wrote him a remarkable letter. He said he was sorry for what had happened. And he

Children

added, "I am sorry I did not room with you again this year. Perhaps I could have helped." It was a "quaint deed," but it was glorious. Not many of us from the adult world are capable of such—we who in such large numbers could not understand why Dean Acheson did not turn his back on a friend when his friend was convicted of perjury. "Keep true to the dreams of thy youth."

Some years ago—not soon enough but still some years ago—Wooster, like many other schools in its part of the world, admitted its first Negro students. At the time one trustee resigned in protest, though later he came back. A few parents had some remarks of mild inquiry. One mother of a new applicant, upon meeting a Negro student in the hall, promptly withdrew her son's application. Wooster is in New England, so none of this is surprising. All that is surprising is that there should have been any protest or murmuring at all. However, the one corner from which there really was no trouble at all was from the students themselves. One boy, in asking if he could room with one of the Negros said, "It is good to have some democratic ideas, but it is more important to live a democratic experience." Most adolescents are more democratic than their parents.

But perhaps I grow too serious. The adult world has much to say about the lack of courtesy among adolescents, and surely there is a lot of evidence to support the charge. Nevertheless, the most polite human I ever knew was an adolescent. Once on a certain sunny afternoon in May the Wooster baseball team was trailing the visiting team by two runs and it was the last half of the ninth inning. There were two outs and Wooster had a man on second and third. The batter hit a ground ball out toward second. The man on third headed for the plate. The catcher was blocking the base path. The throw arrived with the runner, who slid into the catcher, knocking the ball out of his hands. The first man was safe and the second runner was dashing toward home. But the first runner jumped to his feet, picked up the ball, and, handing it to the catcher, said, "I'm very sorry. I didn't mean to bump into you." The umpire promptly called the second man out, ruling interference from the first. The game was over and Wooster had lost. The coach, of course, was furious, and rightly so, since obviously the only way to control sportsmanship in American games is to have rules against it. This boy had broken a rule. There are times, believe it or not, when adolescents can even be more *polite* than the so-called adult world. "Keep true to the dreams of thy youth."

So now at last, what *is* an adolescent? Is he a centaur or a dreamer of dreams. Is he half animal or all man, indeed the most glorious age of man? Who knows? It depends. Perhaps, more than anything else an adolescent is like wine—some good, some bad, and occasionally some plain vinegar. Which it shall be is determined by a variety of things—the soil, the vine, and the grapes. And the weather. These are its heritage. The wine has no control over any of them. If any of them is bad, you shouldn't blame the wine—though with both adolescents and wine, that is just what most of us do. Much, too, depends on the loving care of the vintner: how he tends to the crop, how he makes the wine, how it is barreled and bottled. It also depends on the year.

Descriptions of wine, like descriptions of music and painting, have always amused me. These are things—

Children

perhaps like adolescents too—which simply cannot be captured by words, though the best attempts are delightful. Alexis Lichine describes different vintage years with words which might well be used to describe your children and mine during their different vintage years:

"Slightly on the hard side and will mature slowly."

"A very great year; well adapted to the United States."

"Pessimistic forecasters will have to eat their words."

"Although on the thin side, and very light, they will be pleasant."

"Magnificently balanced, although maturing early." (Here I must call attention to the word "although." Among adolescents there are paragons and Eagle Scouts and acolytes whose parents are inordinately proud of them, not realizing that they have mistaken for permanent virtue what is nothing but early maturity.)

"The future greatness of these wines well warrants the present price." (Here, if I may return to the theme of this book, is a statement of faith!)

Some semi-connoisseurs judge wine by the name. The label does often serve as a helpful hint, though it is not an infallible guide. The connoisseur judges by the individual bottle, knowing that behind some famous labels are some very indifferent wines and that behind some quite unheard-of labels are some magnificently pleasant surprises.

But the super-connoisseur judges by the individual glass. And he will tell you that the last glass from any bottle is better than the first. Why? Because by the time the last glass is drunk he himself may have mellowed a little and (Hear this!) the wine has had a chance to breathe!

Children

I have at times become quite annoyed with lawyers. It seems to me that often their procedure is first to persuade me that what I thought was a rather simple situation—which I almost might have been able to handle myself with a little common sense—is really very difficult and complicated and that I cannot possibly get on without their help. Now I must confess that so far in this discussion I have been using just the methods I deplore when lawyers use them with me. The discussion of death may have been something of an exception; like being sued, it is a moment when most people admit they need a little help. But, fearing that the need might not be so obvious with marriage and the rearing of children, I have labored the point (perhaps too much) that both are immensely complicated and difficult and that most of the world surely does need help. I believe it does. To guide, nurture, understand, and at times even to love one's children seems to me to try every facet of a parent's talent and character. I am persuaded, in fact, like any good lawyer, that the job simply cannot be done adequately alone. I believe that faith is needed. And further, I believe that it is effective.

If the rearing of children is as involved as I think it is and the relationship between parents and their offspring as delicate as I think it is, then being a good parent takes patience and courage and trust and love and humility and perspective and forgiveness—all in degrees and quantities which most parents, of themselves, just do not seem to me to have sufficiently ready to hand. If I were allowed just one single bit of advice to give to parents about their children, I would say, "Pray for them."

Nor is this, I think, a counsel of desperation—except

when it is sought in desperation. Prayer introduces a third Person, with the same salutary effect in the rearing of children as in getting married. And what is needed more than anything else is a third Person. How else does a parent avoid making himself judge and jury, cop and prison warden—a combination which he will not tolerate for a moment in any other area of life? The simple biological fact of having produced a child does not automatically endow any father or mother with any special wisdom or character or even pure love. How is it, then, that a parent suddenly *feels* qualified wholly to direct the life of another human? It may be simply because there is no one to stop him, except perhaps his spouse. (And incidentally, that parents disagree or even fight about how their children should be brought up, is not *necessarily* bad. It would be much worse for them always to agree—and perhaps always be wrong. Harmony is not everything.) Grandparents might help. But in our society they are by blind tradition eliminated as being too old, old-fashioned, and foolish, a terrible misconception most of the time. Very strong teachers can sometimes help, but not often. That leaves it to God. He can help and does—but only when He is consulted.

When a parent prays for his child, he thereby admits that he needs help. And that is good. He also admits that beyond the conflict of wills in the family there is another will which is neither his nor his child's. And that is good. It might even happen that the parent's example might lead his child to pray for him. And that would be good. In the process of prayer, passions are often tamed a little. And that too is good.

We are all shocked at the awesome picture of Abraham, his hand held high, preparing to sacrifice his own son to God. I am sure it is right for us to be shocked. The ancient author of the story meant that we should be. Fortunately, in our day we do not go in much for sacrificing our children in just that way. But there are other things Abraham might have done. He might have sacrificed God to his son. As a matter of fact, God's test was to see whether or not he would be willing to do just that. Most of us would, being smaller than Abraham. He might also have sacrificed his son to himself, leaving God out of it altogether. In our day we practice this kind of human sacrifice more than we are willing to admit. How many prominent and highly successful men are there in the world today whose children have turned out very badly? What happened?

Still another thing Abraham might have done was to sacrifice himself to his son. Does parenthood demand this? I do not know. I hope not. I think not. But it is not the worst of the alternatives. I know a man whose career has been absolutely undistinguished, educationally, financially, and by all the other measures that society normally uses. But he has one glorious accomplishment: he is the father of two of the most distinguished young men I have ever known. I once heard him say, without a trace of bitterness, "I never had a chance to do what I wanted. I had too many responsibilities."

The significant point of the story of Abraham and Isaac, however, is that none of the alternatives that Abraham might have chosen did in fact prove necessary. "For now I know that thou fearest God, seeing thou hast not withheld thy son, thine only son, from me." So it turned out that Abraham had quite a place in history—and so did Isaac, his son—and so did God. "With God all things are possible."

Whatever one may think of the political ideas of Dean Acheson, John Foster Dulles, and Dean Rusk, it must be admitted that they all three have had distinguished careers, and that they have demonstrated a high sense of service and admirable qualities of character. Is it, do you suppose, sheer coincidence that all three were brought up in religious households—the sons of clergy? Recently I went through the entire list of some hundreds of Wooster School boys whom I have known and most of whose parents I have also known. I picked out seventeen whose subsequent lives seemed to me to have been distinguished in terms of moral fibre, service to their fellow man and general meaningfulness. Every one of them came from a home where there was a framework of religious belief and practice—some Protestant, some Roman Catholic, and some Jewish. I know this constitutes no "proof" of anything; I admit I had a tendency to load the dice. But still I think that the pattern is so consistent that it takes quite a bit of explaining away.

"When I was a boy of fourteen," Mark Twain is supposed to have said, "my father was so ignorant I could hardly stand to have the old man around. But when I got to be twenty-one, I was astonished at how much he had learned in seven years." Of course everyone assumes that Mark Twain was joking; what he *really* meant was that *he* had learned a lot in seven years. But I am not sure. Maybe, being a rather sly fellow, Mark Twain meant precisely what he said. I do not know anything about his father, but maybe he really did learn a lot during those seven years, perhaps a great

Children

deal more than his son. Certainly there is much for a parent to learn, not knowledge so much as wisdom. He needs to learn patience and courage and trust and love and humility and perspective and forgiveness. If a parent learns to pray for his child, God may provide him with just these. For prayer is not merely a psychological exercise. It is an appeal for help. I believe that such appeals are heeded.

Moods

Somewhere in most boarding school catalogues there is a picture of the headmaster with a group of the boys. Usually he is standing or sitting in front of a fireplace, smoking a pipe and perhaps wearing a tweed sports coat, with one leather-patched elbow on the mantlepiece. Or he may be leaning forward in his chair, beaming down upon the eager, upturned faces of his little group of students. What the picture is intended to say, regardless of the caption, is, "Here at Farnumdale we are just one big happy family." Summer camps make the same sort of pitch, only the camp mantlepiece is made of rough fieldstone and the director is wearing his letter and maybe a whistle. There are some college catalogues which try it too, with beautiful coeds scattered decoratively about. There are even a few large corporations which through their personnel departments disseminate information designed to persuade potential employees that working for that company is to be a member of the same proverbial one big happy family. Just why, incidentally, the family should be the

Moods

particular social unit designated by custom to epitomize the apogee of perfection in human relations I have never quite understood. I live in a big family, and it is a reasonably happy one. Still I do not think it would quite qualify as the perfect model for perfect human relations.

In any case, everyone knows that such saccharine publicity about the blissful conditions prevailing at schools, colleges, camps, or corporations is false. People live in groups and whether the group is based on ties of blood, belief, or business, the individuals in it face the same life-long problem: getting along together—happily if possible—but, if not, *just getting along at all!* The adjustment to the presence of others is crucial. So many of the other problems in any kind of human institution would either disappear altogether, or be greatly lessened, if it were not for the constant grinding and grating of one personality upon another, the endless friction which is so likely to exist whenever two or three or more humans are gathered together.

A first cause of the problem, I am persuaded, is the selfishness of most people about their moods. We are all so insistent upon letting others know how we feel. It is so foolish, since the very passion of our insistence is all the evidence we need that no one else really cares how we feel. An old sea captain once said, "Never tell your troubles to anyone else. Half the world doesn't give a damn and the other half is glad of it." Nevertheless we continue to go about inflicting our moods on the world, even though experience has again and again demonstrated that all we can hope to get in exchange is abuse.

The way we nurture our moods and the way we assert

them is silly. But it is more than silly. It is a problem
in our lives, the source of a great deal of harm. As
problems, moods would hardly seem comparable to
death and marriage and the rearing of children. Perhaps at first glance moods seem too unimportant to
merit serious consideration in relation to faith. I think
not. In the first place, as I have already intimated, moods
are intricately woven into all of the other situations
we have discussed and will be discussing. It is surely
obvious that anyone, by whatever power, who is able
to preserve an outward serenity in spite of his troubles
or sorrows or pique has some contribution to make to
any situation involving, for example, death or marriage or the rearing of children. Secondly, it is part of
the very foundation, indeed a cornerstone, of my thesis
here, that nothing is too slight or too mundane to be
worthy of the touch of faith's grace. The more mundane, the more specifically is it the business of religion.
So the control of one's moods—a marvelous contribution
to the earth's good when achieved—is important. Being
important, it is the business of belief. And is, to grind
the axe some more, susceptible to religion's ministrations.

Selfishness is at the root of mood trouble. However,
great a man's generosity in other areas of life, he is a
rare person indeed who can be generous about the way
he feels. Most of us have built within us a persistent
urge to make those near us feel the way we feel, good
or bad. It starts early. Nothing quite so thoroughly
infuriates an unhappy or disappointed child as the
gaiety of others. Whenever one of my sons comes under
discipline—which with three boys in the family is fairly
often—my daughter for some reason finds it impossible

to keep a bit of a smirk from her lips. It never fails to send the boys into absolute towers of rage. Only recently have they learned to put the situation to good use by attacking their sister with such vehemence as to drive all thought of their own crimes out of everyone's mind. The final result is that everyone is miserable. And that makes the disciplined boy happy.

If a child's parents are thoroughly enjoying the company of friends and it is time for that child to go to bed, he will not be satisfied simply to be miserable himself about having to go to bed. He will work on the situation with all of the ingenuity God gave him, until finally everyone else is miserable too. Then he will be happy. And he will remember. He will remember the technique, and use it, for the rest of his life—on his friends, his wife, his children, and his children's children.

Man's tendencies toward possessiveness about things is proverbial. But he is seldom half so possessive about his things as he is about his feelings. However he feels, that's the way he wants to feel, and he is likely to resent any attempt to shake him out of his mood, however inappropriate to the occasion it may be, however jarring or offensive to his neighbor.

The first thing in the morning is a good time to study this mood-cuddling phenomenon. Our morning moods are so ill concealed; they are so varied; and each of us is so very jealous about the way he feels. This classic exchange illustrates the point. "Good morning!" "What's good about it?" Probably the cheerful soul is as guilty as the sourpuss. Both, after all, have the same selfish motive. "I want you to feel the way I feel. At least I don't want you trying to change the way I feel." Most of

the time, the words "Cheer up!" are the most useless
words one can utter. Almost inevitably they produce
an effect exactly opposite to the one desired.

By contrast, anyone who can somehow achieve an
outward serenity regardless of how he feels within, who
can be calm in the midst of troubled seas, who can manage to say just the right word instead of just the wrong
word in a time of crisis—or no word at all—such a one
truly is worth his weight in gold in any family or in any
other human situation. It is, I think, no mere chance
that sainthood and serenity so often go together. When
the truth is known, forms of greatness other than saintliness are often marred by scars—sometimes life scars—
that the great have left on those closest to them. So a
prophet is not without honor save in his own home.
But it is the peculiar blessing of the special sainthood
of serenity that it is usually and properly, indeed especially, honored at home.

It is worthwhile to remind ourselves that the devil
never misses a chance to spoil good by any means. So
sometimes such saintliness in one heart actually en-
genders envious fury in others. An easily perturbable
doctor, after years of silent suffering, at last confessed
to a patient of his who had become his close friend that
he had hated him in the early days of their acquaintance just because of the patient's apparent imperturb-
ability. The doctor was absolutely delighted, therefore,
to discover one day that the patient had an ulcer. It
was the real beginning of their friendship. What the
doctor had thought was a natural gift—therefore unfair
and infuriating—had been, it turned out, an inward
struggle not unlike his own. Jealousy gave way to admiration, and friendship, so long stunted in the shade,

could at last grow and blossom in the sun. We all admire self-control in the abstract. It is a pity we cannot admire it more when we find it concrete in a neighbor's heart. Ourselves possessed, we perversely turn against the self-possessed our ridicule and scorn, calling good evil and strength weakness.

We aspire, but our achievements are often disappointingly meager and distressingly temporary. Life can be cruel, and there are times when irritability seems almost forgivable. Everyone has his breaking point.

One Monday morning a few summers ago, I took the train from Cape Cod, where we were vacationing, to New York. My wife and I drove to the station with our four children, I (like many another commuter in this world) hiding my glee at the thought of some peaceful hours on the train and a few days of work I secretly greatly enjoyed behind the fraudulent façade of duty artfully contrived to reveal just enough of the cares of the breadwinner and the debilitating heat of the city. My wife was very sad that morning, not because I was leaving, but because she was staying, "trapped," as she said, with those four horrible children. As we waited at the station, another car drove up, also containing a husband (hiding his gaiety a little less well than I, I thought) and a wife and four children. Like a stereopticon slide, this double vision suddenly came into focus for me, and my heart was touched by a sentiment which I took to be pity—though born not so much of compassion as of guilt. To cover my embarrassment, I jocularly suggested to the other mother that she and my wife swap children for the week. (It might have helped a little.) The husband laughed nervously and his wife smiled wanly. My wife looked daggers. We

Moods

two Adams boarded the train and as it pulled out, we waved goodbye, too little cursed, but having at least won the sympathy of our children. The Eves, self-sympathy smouldering in their breasts, turned on their heels as though crushing serpents and walked away. As the train wended its way down to New York, on every station platform the scene was duplicated—two or three or four screaming brats waving madly at a grinning father while a poor, pathetic, already beaten mother stood limply with her brood. At New London one mother was pregnant besides. By the time I got to New York I was nearly in tears, my heart bleeding for the mothers of the Eastern seaboard. Life can be cruel. And those husbands, returning Friday evening, should not be too surprised to find their wives slightly irritable.

There are times, I say, when irritability *almost* seems forgivable. But never quite. It is too devastating ever to be the right answer to any situation on earth. It is a deadly weapon, wielded too often and too irresponsibly, without any clear realization of the damage it can do. And the damage can be extreme.

Not long ago I was visited by a young man in his late twenties whom I had known when he was a schoolboy. I had not seen him in some years and he began to tell me something about his life. He had been working as a sales manager for an appliance dealer. The idea had been that he would eventually buy into the firm and be a partner. This plan sounded pretty good for a young fellow. "But," he said, "it didn't work out. He and I just didn't get along. Now I think I will move out and try to get a job with a large corporation, where individual personalities cannot upset things too much." Of course he is a spoiled fool, spoiled because at that point he was indulging himself by simply escaping an unpleasant situation and a fool because it was perfectly evident that moving out wasn't going to make any difference at all. Personalities will always upset things, in any human organization of whatever size, unless the people with the difficult personalities—and who hasn't one?—do something about themselves. Moving elsewhere doesn't do any good, and for most of the world it isn't even possible. Most marriages that are weakened or wounded or wrecked are so because one or the other or both parties insist upon sharing not their joys and their hopes and their sorrows and their fears, but merely their pique, their irritation, their downright cussedness and their black bile.

The story, of course, is a very ancient one. Cain killed Abel partly because he didn't like the mood his brother was in. Cain was feeling sorry for himself, and he just couldn't stand the sight of anyone who wasn't feeling the same way. Misery loves company, but does not graciously consort with any but its own kind. The Bible is full of stories of people who had trouble controlling their moods. The language of the Bible on this subject seems archaic to us now but the problem then was the same as it is today. I have a strong feeling that even the language, however archaic, still has something to say that is pertinent. They spoke in those days of "being possessed," of "unclean spirits," and of "evil spirits." And they spoke, more realistically than we, of "exorcism," that is, of the driving out of such spirits. The implication was that it could and should be done.

The story of King Saul seems rather relevant because he was a particularly cantankerous fellow, who, like

many moody men in places of high authority, was especially selfish about the way he felt. Those around him,
partly from fear no doubt, but also from solicitude, were
usually inclined to do what they could to help the situation—like really good secretaries coping with surly
bosses on Monday mornings.

One thing that could be said for these ancients is
that they recognized the problem; their diagnosis was
sound. On one memorable occasion they said of Saul,
"The spirit of the Lord has departed from him." Or, as
we would say—in an occasional burst of charity—"He
is not himself." That diagnosis was correct, but their
solution to the problem was less so. They called in
David, a comely youth who played the harp and sang
pretty well. How often we have tried to solve the problem in the same way. Pleasant companionship and a
little soft music. It sometimes works for a while, but
never for long, for it does not really get at the heart
of the matter, which is within us, not outside us. And
so, one fine day when David was playing soothing music
to the petulant king, Saul got so mad that he grabbed
a spear and threw it at the boy—a fearsome forerunner
of the dirty look across the top of the morning newspaper in reply to a well-meaning pleasantry at the
breakfast table.

In the country of the Gadarenes, Jesus once performed a miracle. He cured a man who was possessed
of an unclean spirit, driving the spirit into some swine
which were near at hand. The story is well-known, but
there are two phrases in it which I believe merit special
attention. When the man confronted Jesus and asked
Him for help, Jesus' first words were, "Come out of the
man, thou unclean spirit." This underlines again the

point brought out in the story of Saul and David. There are times when we are, in a sense, truly "possessed." Psychiatry today has fancy names for such conditions, but in our everyday language we tend more to hark back to the ancients. When we have behaved very badly, we say, "I don't know what got into me."

Jesus, standing in front of the man, spoke directly, not to the man but to the spirit that possessed him. One can imagine what an effect this simple beginning must have had on the man. Jesus believed in him. He knew that what possessed the man was not the same thing as his self. And when Jesus spoke to the evil spirit as a separate entity, the man must have known that his release was at hand. It was good for him to know that the two were not the same.

The superficial friendships with which our society abounds are shown for what they are by the ease and speed by which they are so often dissolved—sometimes after five or ten years of existence, sometimes only because of a single unfortunate incident or passionate outburst. Now and then we have the compassion to say, "This was not like him. Something must be eating him." But too often we say instead, "Well, if that's the kind of guy he is, I want nothing more to do with him. I'm glad I finally found out the truth about him." Jesus said, "Come out of the man, thou unclean spirit."

It is a blessing that in recent years so much light has been shed on the subject of alcoholism and alcoholics. Now we call the addiction a disease and separate it from the person. Why can we not do the same for other people, often far less afflicted, but afflicted nevertheless? "Stay yourselves, and wonder;" wrote Isaiah, "cry ye out, and cry: they are drunken, but not with wine;

they stagger, but not with strong drink." Whether we are dealing with our own moods or the moods of others, it is good to know that the unclean spirit and the self are not the same. Nevertheless, in dealing with our own moods we must realize that if the unclean spirit *does* indeed possess us, the outward result is the same as if the demon were our self. We must be rid of him. And here Jesus was more wise than the friends of Saul.

His next question, again addressed to the spirit, was, "What is thy name?" I have spoken elsewhere of the ancient Hebrew legend which says that, if one is able to identify a spirit, to call it by name, one will also be able to have some influence over it. Here again the legend is pertinent. I believe that we could often control the evil spirits which possess us if we could or would only call them by their right names. We all have our little list of names we like. Tired. Overworked. Under-Great-Strain (one of those English hyphenated names). Put-upon. Cheated (a great favorite among the young). Unlucky. Then there is another list of names which we all hate—usually a much longer list, and sometimes indeed those names are legion. Hungover. Selfish. Petulant. Jealous. Hotheaded. Lazy. Thoughtless. Rude. How many times might the evil spirits which possess us be more easily exorcised if we were only wise enough or honest enough or brave enough to call them by their right names!

Living as I do on the campus of a boarding school which prepares all of its students for admission to American colleges and universities, I am provided each spring with a particularly poignant opportunity to observe how fiendishly young men can at times be possessed. The news of acceptance or rejection by the

Moods

various institutions of higher learning generally arrives for most boys at more or less the same time—some of it good and some of it bad, all of it of great moment. Naturally the selfishness of feelings is all but unquenchable. And because of the pressures, this is understandable. How can one persuade a boy whose dreams of years have been realized not to rejoice too much in the presence of his roommate, whose news was bad? Or, more difficult, how can one persuade the roommate not to spoil the other's moment of joy by being too gloomy? It is, perhaps, asking too much of either. Nevertheless, and therefore, how glorious is the sight when one of them is able to reach such heights of grace. At such a moment it seems to me fairly certain that someone has been using some right names, calling spades spades, and considering himself lucky, rather than virtuous, to have drawn an ace.

Whether we are dealing with the moods of others or with our own—and life gives us plenty of opportunity to practice with each—it is important, I think, to remember both of the phrases which Jesus used in addressing himself to the unclean spirit. Our tendency is to remember only one—depending upon whether we are dealing with our own moods or those of others. With ourselves, "Come out of the man" makes a lot of sense. We may say, "I don't know what possessed me." But we are sure enough that it was something not of our self. The name escapes us. When we are dealing with someone else, we have no trouble finding the right names. "He's just a selfish, hotheaded fool!" But we lack the charity to see the separateness. In *both* instances *both* phrases, and the concepts they embody, are necessary.

Moods

One of the fascinating things about the miracle that Jesus did in the country of the Gadarenes is the fear expressed by the unclean spirit. "What have I to do with thee, Jesus, thou Son of the most high God? I adjure thee by God, that thou torment me not." We are so used to thinking of the unclean spirits which possess us as the tormentors that it does not occur to us that they can themselves be tormented and driven out. Perhaps we allow them to feel too much at home in us. Evil spirits play games with us. Why cannot we play games with them? Is subtlety a weapon available only to the devil? The members of Alcoholics Anonymous know enough not to take the pledge except a day at a time. For some it works pretty well. One day follows another. Could not other temptations to self-indulgence, including our treasured moods, be treated in the same way? Of course it is not easy. Prayer becomes part of the procedure—not self-hypnosis but prayer, the actual seeking for help outside ourselves, in the sure and certain hope that there shall be an answer.

What is behind it all, our so-serious clinging to our moods, *insisting* that they—and we—be taken seriously? It is our constant fear that we may be thought a fool, or of no account. And so, given rope enough, we become fools, just to prove that we are not. So from nothing, something ogrish is born!

To temper, says the dictionary, means "to bring to the desired consistency, texture, degree of toughness, as clay by wetting and kneading, steel or glass by gradual heating and cooling, or artists' colors by mixing with oil . . . in music to tune; especially to adjust the pitch of (a note, chord, instrument, or the like) to a temperament." Usually we talk only about losing our temper and we tend to assume that when we do not lose our temper everything is all right. Perhaps we should think more often of the other meaning. In fact, anyone who has achieved a real temper in his life has achieved a great deal. It is a beautiful and delicate balance of the spirit. As with a musical instrument there is need for constant adjustment. It is not something which is done once and for all. The instrument changes with the weather and with age. It may have to be adjusted differently for different kinds of music. Occasionally it may even be necessary for it to be tuned just a little less than perfectly in order to harmonize with other instruments less delicate. Can it be that this is too mundane or picayune a matter to be worthy of the help of God? How could it be so? Is it not in truth the Kingdom of God within us?

Happiness

Following a discussion of moods, a discourse on happiness would seem to be an invitation to repetition and redundance. It is true that the two subjects have a lot in common, that they are closely allied and so are often confused. Still, I think they are different and therefore should be treated separately. Happiness is more a state of being, not uninterrupted, to be sure, but still not so ever-changing as a mood, which often is nothing more than a reflection of a moment. Happiness is commonly thought of as a goal to be pursued (though I think this is partly wrong), while a mood (good or bad) is usually felt as something that grips and pursues us, more or less in spite of ourselves. Generally speaking, we tend to shrug our shoulders about moods and to say there is really nothing much we can do about them. But we think of happiness as our birthright and something for which we should constantly fight.

Perhaps the basic different between moods and happiness could be better understood if we were able simply to reverse the common conception of what the two actually are. But to clarify that statement it will be necessary to have some understanding of just what happiness is. Let us, therefore, start with some traditional symbols.

The soft purr of a cat, snuggled warmly in a corner of the living room couch in front of a gently burning fire of a winter's evening; a puppy, madly wagging his tail, as his young master holds out a biscuit for him; a cow, standing in the shade of an ancient maple tree on a hot summer's day, chewing her cud and flapping flies with ears and tail; a clam at high tide! Among men these are accepted symbols of happiness and contentment, though just how man came to know that these fellow creatures are happy under such circumstances I am not sure. Alice in Wonderland is one of the few people I know who ever bothered to ask, and from the Cheshire Cat she got a rather inconclusive answer. By a bit of severe logic in his answer, he merely proved to Alice that he was mad. "To begin with," said the Cat, "a dog's not mad. You grant that? . . . Well, then, you see a dog growls when it's angry, and wags its tail when it's pleased. Now *I* growl when I'm pleased, and wag my tail when I'm angry. Therefore I'm mad." And nothing, meanwhile, was said about the famous grin, which apparently signified nothing. The fact remains, however, that to most men the cat and the dog and the cow and the clam, each under the circumstances described above, suggest happiness. And, looking at these fortunate creatures, man envies them their enjoyment of a state of being so greatly to be desired.

What is alarming is that man should so preoccupy himself with the search and struggle for the kind of happiness he imagines exists in the hearts of these fellow creatures. Not a few among us feel that the pursuit of such is the whole purpose and justification of human life. Some presume to think it is their *right* and are annoyed at Life or Fate or God—whoever happens to be nearest at hand at the moment—if they are not provided with what they consider their due measure. If indeed we did have a right to a certain definite portion of carefree animal ease, we should have to charge God (or Life or Fate) with a pretty badly botched-up job, since only a tiny minority of humans ever manage such comfort or contentment, except in very short spurts—and a very tiny minority of animals too, for that matter. After all, if the clam is happy only at high tide, he is unhappy a good deal of the time. In such light, the presumptuousness of a person's *demand* for happiness as a *right* is staggering. To most of the rest of the world it is also offensive.

As with so many other human situations, the issue is not so hard to understand as long as we look at it as it affects someone else. From the perspective of such detachment we notice an interesting thing. When a human is very young, we are really quite sympathetic toward his desire for, and interpretation of, happiness. We do not blame him for seeing it simply in terms of a warm bottle and dry diapers, nor for crying when he wants them and gurgling when he gets them. Until he is three, perhaps, we continue to acknowledge that a little cuddling and an occasional candy still are excusable and natural. But our patience passes as the child grows older. There comes a time sooner or later when we are taking pot shots with a double-barrelled, emotion-loaded gun. With one barrel we fire off our resentment at the notion that such snivelling upstarts should have any right to the happiness they continue to demand for themselves. And with the other we release volleys of irate demands that, if they want happiness so badly, why don't they go out and make their own? This last is particularly prevalent during the weeks of summer vacation, when the challenge to the young to "be happy" is often so insistently presented by parents that they can see no way that it could be ducked except by sheer juvenile cussedness. Thus, when this challenge *is* ducked, parents quickly attribute the failure to absolute perversity and figuratively stalk off in a rage, leaving no happiness anywhere, except the cheap tidbit that they may try to salvage by assuring themselves that they, at least, have a clear conscience.

In my own life there is another interpretation of happiness which I find even more infuriating. As everyone knows, one of the pressure points in America today is in the area of higher education. Getting accepted by a reputable institution is difficult, and those who succeed are exceedingly fortunate. But again, as everyone knows, acceptance is not the end of the process. We are told that over 50 per cent of all those entering colleges and universities in the United States today never finish. I have talked to a great many who dropped out, trying to find out what went wrong. The most common answer I get—and it is offered so blandly and matter-of-factly! —is, "I just wasn't happy there, and so I saw no point in sticking it out." This is nothing short of blasphemy, and there follows a duel of eyes—who can open his the widest in wonder. "What's wrong with that?" cries one set. "You can't be serious!" says the other.

Up to this point, we, the detached observers, can clearly see what is wrong. Consciously or unconsciously, our sympathy has dwindled in a line declining in exact ratio with the baby's development from an infant to a man. So we say with ire and impatience, if not with reason, "You can't expect to be happy like an animal is happy all your life! You are no longer an animal. With humans it is different, and the sooner you learn that the better." But how is the poor child to learn? He has been too long and too well tutored by another generation (his parents') that animal happiness, cud-chewing, tail-wagging happiness—is real happiness. He has been taught by what he has been offered in the name of happiness. Long after the bottle and the dry diapers, there was the bicycle and the car, for who can be happy except on the move? He has also been tutored by example. For we, the detached, so often fail entirely to understand for ourselves what we preach to others. We too would fain chew our cud to nourish our soul.

The cud, incidentally, is a more appropriate symbol than may at first appear. It represents the quintessence of self-indulgence. When a cow chews her cud, she is doing no one any good but herself. And besides, the very thing she chews is part of herself, something she ate before, no less! One cannot blame the poor cow. She doesn't know any better. For her this is the only kind of happiness there is. But, when a man tries it, he fails. The trouble is that he simply is not built like a cow. All he can get from chewing his cud is indigestion.

It is a pity that the perspective with which we can so clearly see others, especially a younger generation, is difficult to use on ourselves. So the happiness we seek, at any age, is so often elusive because it is illusory. It is the same as that sought by the very young, only now we are not very young, nor are we cows.

Happiness

In the cleverness of their years, grown men are able to find a far greater variety of cuds with which to indulge and delude themselves than they could when they were younger. There are games and there are things. There are shows and libations. There are status symbols, inclusions and exclusions—fences to be on the right side of. When he waxes poetic, man says to himself, "All I want is a loaf of bread, a jug of wine and thou!" Who wants to be a cow? Just ask the cow to move over and give us a little room under the same maple tree.

It sounds delightful, but there may be flies, and it may rain, and the bread and wine may give out. However delightful, this obviously cannot be a way of life, but at best only an interlude of self-indulgence. Even the presence of the "thou" is for "my" sake, not for "thine." Man's pursuit of happiness is thus greatly marred (like that of his sons and daughters) by his failure to understand what it is, where it may be found, and what its proper place in life ought to be. If most men find happiness elusive, therefore, it is at least partly because they wouldn't know it if they saw it.

Perhaps we should start by recognizing what happiness is *not*. In theatrical parlance there is a kind of play called "situation comedy." Though many of us appear to believe in, and search for, "situation happiness," there is no such thing. For happiness is not dependent upon the nature of a situation. Too easily do we blame the events and circumstances of our lives. If only this condition or that state of affairs could be changed, we tell ourselves, all would be well. However familiar, the story of the American soldier's week end with an English duke and duchess is particularly appropriate. When asked what sort of time he had had, he said, "Well, it was an *iffy* week end. If the water had been as cold as the soup; and if the soup had been as warm as the wine; and if the wine had been as old as the chicken; and if the chicken had been as tender as the maid; and if the maid had been as willing as the duchess—I wouldn't be home yet." It is easy to be deluded into thinking that, if only a given situation were a little different, we could be happy.

At this point, of course, envy and covetousness become the devil's first lieutenants. If only we had as much money as our neighbors on the left . . . if only our children were as bright as our neighbors' on the right . . . if only my husband had a job that kept him home more like my neighbor's across the street . . . if only we had a house (or a car or a boat) like our neighbors' around the corner. *If only.* Both words are misleading. *If* suggests that something in a given situation has to change and *then* happiness would be within our grasp. *Only* suggests that just *one* thing has to change and all will be well.

Of course situations do have a bearing. In some circumstances happiness is admittedly easier to achieve than in others. But I do not believe that the situation is ever the determining factor in achieving human happiness. It does make a difference to the person who is seeking only contentedness—the contentedness of a cow. If that is what happiness is for man, then what he needs is a cud to chew, and a warm summer day, and a tail to drive away the flies, and the shade of a maple tree. Albert Einstein once said, "Happiness is for pigs." I doubt that he would want to argue the difference between a cow and a pig, but I hope that what he meant to say was simply that pig happiness is for pigs, as cow happiness is for cows.

I believe that human happiness is something quite different, different in many ways, but most importantly different in its freedom from dependence upon comforts, conveniences, events, circumstances, and situations. The truly and genuinely and properly happy people on this earth are never slaves to the longing cry, "if only." Their happiness is within them, of their own making, a response to, rather than a result of, what happens and what happens to be.

A retired teacher who was more than seventy years old and who had spent forty years teaching came out of retirement for a term to help at a school that was in a difficult situation. One gray February day he burst into the faculty room during a mid-morning recess, and pounding his palm with his fist, he said, "Gee, I love to teach!" A young colleague with a total of four years' experience in the profession looked up from his newspaper and said laconically, "Son, wait till you've tried it a couple of years." It was intended and taken as a bit of byplay, but every man in the room felt a twinge of envy and admiration in his heart, knowing that the older man had found something more rare than the fountain of youth. He had found the fountain of joy, which makes the fountain of youth seem strangely irrelevant and needless. Let those who fight for higher teachers' salaries across the land—and I have done it myself—bear in mind that this enthusiasm has no price.

Such joy, of course, is as far removed from cud-chewing happiness as can be. Indeed, in every way it is its very opposite. The difference is like the difference between the pleasure a child gets from eating a piece of

cake and the pleasure his mother gets in baking it for
him. When Jesus said, "It is more blessed to give than
to receive," he meant not only that it is more praise-
worthy, though it is that. He meant also that it is more
fun, that it is more delightful, and more refreshing.
Refreshing is perhaps the best word of all, for it describes quite precisely what happens inside a man when
he gives. The physical act of making love is an apt
analogy. To be sure, there are satisfactions for one's self,
but it is well known that these satisfactions are greatest
in direct proportion to the joy that is given. If part of the
intention and result is to create new life, then this is
indeed the final blessing and the perfect symbol of
proper human happiness. We humans presume to believe
that this particular blessing is reserved for us, that no
animal can know of all the nuances of human love, most
particularly of the conscious giving of joy and the conscious creating of life. If we are right, then we are
blessed peculiarly. Happiness for us is something
unique, that exists only within us.

If human happiness is not dependent upon circumstances, it is also something which cannot be caught by
being pursued. It is, instead, a by-product of a certain
kind and quality of life. It is never a goal in itself, and
when we try to make it one, it always proves elusive. As
an illustration—no, more as a symbol—consider the golf
ball. At the outset, I must confess my prejudice against
the game of golf, fully realizing that in doing so I offend
potential readers by the millions. I think golf is selfish
and futile. If you happen to be President, or something,
it may be all right as an occasional method for getting
out in the open and exchanging one frustration for
another. But as an obsession, I repeat, it is selfish and

futile. Though the selfishness is extreme and consuming and blinding, what concerns me at the moment is the futility. "In that little white ball," thinks the golfer, "lies my happiness." So he hits it and chases it and hits it and loses it; he replaces it and hits it and polishes it and mars it; and at the end of the day, often in fury, he pockets it and goes home to face a neglected and properly angry wife. The smile on the ball, like the grin on the Cheshire Cat, signifies no joy.

I do not know exactly what our forefathers had in mind when they bracketed the pursuit of happiness with life and liberty. Perhaps we should have the right to pursue happiness in the same sense that Adam and Eve were given the right to eat the forbidden fruit. But we ought to have wisdom enough to know that the pursuit is hopeless. It is exactly as hopeless as to pursue the pot of gold at the end of the rainbow. Only in heart and mind can it be reached, and then only when one's heart and mind are preoccupied with something else, something less self-conscious. We need the faith to believe that all the time we are thrashing about blindfolded, pursuing happiness, it is in fact pursuing us. Sometimes, just because of our gyrations, it finds us hard to locate. I believe, however, that when we are "about our Father's business," happiness will know where to look and will surely catch up to us.

The context of happiness does not have to be specifically religious, though its ultimate validation is. What is important is that we lose ourselves in something, something that will "take us out of the loneliness of self." This, I believe, is the first step toward achieving human happiness, though even this first step must be taken unself-consciously. Probably two of the happiest people

in America are Dr. and Mrs. Frank Boyden, for over
half a century the heads of Deerfield Academy, one of
America's great schools. On the occasion of their fiftieth
anniversary, Dr. Harold Dodds, then President of
Princeton University, wrote the following tribute:
"They are truly dedicated to the service of youth, although, if you were to tell them this to their faces, they
would look embarrassed and self-conscious. Indeed for
them the phrase does seem to be out of proper perspective, for they get far too much fun out of what they are
doing to think of themselves as dedicated to anything.
All they are doing is living happy lives, whereas 'dedi-
cation' somehow suggests an element of self-conscious
martyrdom, or at least self-denial—and you will not find
any trace of either in the Boydens."

This tribute is a veritable patchwork of paradox.
One might almost think that here was a perfect picture
of two people who had spent their whole lives selfishly
doing what would give them the most fun, that the fact
that their lives have been useful to others is nothing
more than fortuitous coincidence. But the patchwork
has a pattern, and the paradox is resolved by the orthodoxy of the ancient precept that, "Whosoever shall lose
his life, for my sake, shall find it." If these two people
were merely selfishly doing what gave them the most
fun, then it *would* be sheer coincidence that others
should benefit from it. But, since their lives have in
fact been dedicated (whether the word embarrasses
them or not) to the service of others, then it is *not*
coincidence that they should be happy. It is part of the
pattern, the orthodox and inevitable pattern of a Christian paradox.

Human happiness, I have said, is not finally dependent upon circumstances; neither can it be caught by being specifically pursued. But even though there may be agreement thus far, there is still one legitimate question which now deserves attention. "Is not happiness," some will ask, "even the most exalted and purest form of human happiness, something of a question of temperament, a natural gift? Is it not, as my father used to say, "a matter of glands?"

In part it must be. It would be ridiculous to maintain that temperament is entirely irrelevant, that there is not a substantial difference in the ease or difficulty with which various people are able to achieve happiness. Just as circumstances do have some bearing and pursuit is relevant, so temperament is certainly a factor. I am sure, nevertheless, that temperament is no more a determining factor than circumstance or pursuit. In assessing the apparent and easy happiness of others, it is always inviting to believe that they were just fortunate to have been born the way they are—and we, poor souls, were unlucky. But we are on dangerous ground when we are too quick to discount the inner struggles of another's soul and to write off great triumphs of the spirit as "natural gifts." If it can be said that circumstances—that is, "situation happiness,"—is not the final determining factor, then it can also be said that temperament is a kind of subtle extension of that, the circumstance of being born with a sunny disposition, for example. Circumstantially, in America, it is usually easier to be happy if you are white than if you are a Negro. Yet color is certainly not the final determining factor in human happiness. No more is temperament—indeed less, for a man, if he will, can do something about his temperament.

Happiness

And "if he will" is precisely the phrase and the point to bear in mind. Surely there are times in the life of every man when his soul is enslaved by misery and frustration and fear and sorrow. Indeed there are times —many times—when to be happy is very inappropriate. But to permit one's soul *always* to be so enslaved is a kind of self-indulgent servility which is properly punished by a joyless life.

Now what are we to say about human happiness and faith? The issue is not clear cut; for the confusion between human happiness and the contentedness of a cow persists. So at first glance it appears that the religious man is not the happiest of men, almost that it is his religion which keeps him from being happy. Certainly John Calvin, John Milton, Martin Luther, and Bernard of Clairvaux—to name a few great religious men more or less at random—are not first thought of as happy men. Even Jesus Christ walked the earth in suffering and sorrow. And most often his disciples suffered with him. Indeed one of the stumbling blocks for the irreligious is that religion seems to them so specifically to exclude happiness, *or at least what they think of as happiness*. And certainly it does. For the unselfish, unself-centered, compassionate man of conscience, most of what passes for happiness among men *is* excluded. How can the rest of the world rejoice as long as one man suffers? Much less, how can one man be happy when much of the rest of the world suffers. The first service of faith in this regard, therefore, is to clarify the issue—to provide a believer with the courage and selflessness and the sensitivity to brush aside almost all of what most of the world considers happiness as being improper and immoral—fit only for pigs. If Jesus Christ suffered more than he rejoiced, it was because mankind just did not know enough or care enough not to rejoice, while their fellows suffered. Their pursuit of happiness was blind. Part of the purpose of the life and teaching and suffering and death of Jesus Christ was to make some believers less blind. And it has.

Still, there is another side to the story. The word joy, it seems to me, is particularly a religious word. And all the literary expressions of the highest of human ecstasy are either religious in their nature or have strong religious overtones. The author of the Hundredth Psalm may be cited as one among very, very many examples of the joyousness of faith.

O be joyful in the Lord, all ye lands: serve the Lord with gladness, and come before his presence with a song. Be ye sure that the Lord he is God; it is he that hath made us, and not we ourselves; we are his people, and the sheep of his pasture. O go your way into his gates with thanksgiving, and into his courts with praise; be thankful unto him, and speak good of his Name. For the Lord is gracious, his mercy is everlasting; and his truth endureth from generation to generation.

And some lines from the preceding psalm:

Show yourselves joyful unto the Lord, all ye lands; sing, rejoice, and give thanks. Praise the Lord upon the harp; sing to the harp with a psalm of thanksgiving. With trumpets also and shawms, O show yourselves joyful before the Lord, the King.

Then, of course, there is St. Francis of Assisi, perhaps the happiest man who ever lived. His whole life was a song of joy, of unquenchable exuberance. He rejoiced in every aspect of God's creation and considered himself kin to it all—not only to his fellow men but to all birds and beasts, and even such things as the sun and moon and fire and water. And yet how different is his description of perfect joy from what we might think of as such. These are said to have been his words on the subject to Brother Leo.

I am returning from Perugia and I am coming here at night, in the dark. It is winter time and wet and muddy and so cold that icicles form at the edges of my habit and keep striking my legs, and blood flows from such wounds. And I come to the gate, all covered with mud and cold and ice, and, after I have knocked and called for a long time, a friar comes and asks: "Who are you?" I answer: "Brother Francis." And he says: "Go away. This is not a decent time to be going about. You can't come in."

And when I insist again, he replies: "Go away. You are a simple and uneducated fellow. From now on don't stay with us any more. We are so many and so important that we don't need you." But still I stand at the gate and say: "For the love of God, let me come in tonight." And he answers: "I won't. Go to the Crosiers' Place and ask there." I tell you that—if I kept patience and was not upset—that is true joy and true virtue and the salvation of the soul."

Thomas à Kempis puts it somewhat differently:

The glory of a good man is the witness of a good conscience. Preserve a quiet conscience, and you will always have joy. . . . You may rest easy if your heart does not reproach you, and you are happy only when you have done right. . . . For the joy of the Saints is from God and in God, and their joy is in the truth. . . . To live inwardly to God, and not to be bound by worldly affections, is the proper state of a spiritual man.

The conclusion to be drawn from all of this is that such happiness as man may properly aspire to can be based only in the glory of God and the successful submission of his own will to God's. It is, in its very essence, religious and moral. The joy that a man may feel for what God has wrought—the sun and moon and stars, and beauty and truth and the goodness of a good man who is only a little lower than the angels—is a proper source of his happiness. So is the joy he feels whenever he subjugates his own will to God's, when he has become submissive to the Almighty and when he has "done right"—provided he can somehow keep the sin of pride from entering just at that moment. If happiness is to wallow in one's own muck, then happiness is for pigs. But the only way to escape from one's own muck is to escape from one's self. So "the joy of Saints is from God and in God."

Human happiness must be human, and to me that implies a spiritual dimension, the hallmark of humanity. As a truly loving husband cannot be happy while his wife is unhappy, so man cannot be happy as a man, while God is unhappy. Man's happiness must be tied to God's. So he can rejoice in whatever is pleasing to God, in the world, in his fellow man and in himself. And he can rejoice in nothing else. This means, of course, that there are limits to his happiness, as there surely must be to God's. To recognize no such limits for one's self—religious or irreligious—this, too, is to be a pig. The man of faith has the humility and the insight and the unselfishness to have some idea what the limits of happiness are.

Furthermore, when those limits have been reached, he knows how to endure. His faith teaches him not only when his own happiness is inappropriate but how to live gracefully without it. Largely it is a matter of harmony—with God, with the lot of his fellow man, and within himself. To achieve harmony everything must be in tune with something, to begin with. A symphony orchestra is usually tuned to the piano, not because it is most surely most nearly right, but because it is the hardest instrument to change in front of all those people during a concert. Often we think of ourselves as the piano and try to tune the rest of the world to ourselves, not because we are most surely most nearly right but because we find ourselves the hardest to change in the midst of life, in front of all those people. The religious man is less likely than others to yield to the temptation of relating all things to himself. And if he does yield, he at least sees to it that his piano is tuned rather regularly by a pitch pipe which is as near to Perfect Pitch as he can manage. He knows that his happiness depends on that—and on nothing else.

Of course this analogy is an invitation for a theological trip around Robin Hood's barn. Where will you find the pipe with Perfect Pitch? And how do you know or decide whether it is the right one? And who are you to decide? And so on and on. But since this is not a theological exercise, I think I can fairly refuse to take that trip. I simply say that there are some people who

Happiness

seem to me to have worked out a satisfactory and sensible and practical answer to these questions. And in large numbers they have (through the centuries) found their answers within the confines of some orthodox, historic, traditional faith. When Jesus said, "I am the Way the Truth and the Life," quite a lot of people believed Him. And to them He further said, "Peace I leave with you, my peace I give unto you: not as the world giveth, give I unto you." As some men have believed that, it has been so for them.

Or would you rather be a pig?

Love

A young lady once turned to me in the middle of a luncheon party and said, "How can I love the Lord with all my heart and all my soul and all my mind? I can't come anywhere near it. Sometimes I don't love Him at all, and often I don't even want to love Him. I just don't feel like trying." The question, it seemed to me, was ill-timed. It was not the sort on which one can elaborate with much success between soup and dessert. I am not sure, as a matter of fact, that it can be elaborated upon with anything but very modest success at any time, under any circumstances.

How to believe: it is a tough question—a little like the scholastic question so popular nowadays—how to study. In the educational field it has always seemed to me that, if you could get a person to understand *why* he should study, he would find out *how*. Of course there are techniques that can be demonstrated, and they can be very helpful. But they are helpful only to those who already *want* to learn, and even then they have to be modified and altered to suit each individual learner. As with the mind, so with the heart. The question of *how* to believe has meaning only after some answers to *why* have aroused a desire. The central purpose of this book is to try to arouse the desire, to make people want to believe, not tell them how.

In the earliest days of Christian history, people in great numbers were attracted to a new faith by the wonderful difference it so evidently seemed to make in the lives of believers. It was not a theological argument but the example of graceful people that drew the converts. Often the case was presented dramatically in an arena with lions. These people seemed to know how to die for what they believed, and naturally it caused many to ask just what that belief was all about. And not only was the way the believers died impressive, but also the way they lived—their morality and their cheerfulness and the general strength of their convictions.

I believe that there are still such people, and that they are still presenting the same kind of evidence about their faith. It is, of course, seldom as dramatic as in the days of the Roman Empire and often not so clear. And, unhappily, the whole picture is sometimes beclouded by charlatans whose gracelessness gives faith a bad name. Still the evidence is abundant, and to me it is convincing. It is better to believe. For anyone who disagrees with that statement, the question of how to believe is frivolous, meaningless, and unanswerable. For the person who agrees that it is truly better to believe, the question *is* answerable, though most of the answer must be worked out by himself. A man once said to Jesus, "Lord, I believe; help mine unbelief." Only in such a spirit can the question of how to believe be approached, and even then without too high hopes for a magic formula.

What is said here is intended for those who may now be ready to ask the question of how to believe in just such a spirit. The answer cannot be a wholly satisfactory one, but it may nevertheless be of some help. Later on we shall return to another aspect of the problem, for the answer, it seems to me, has two parts. One has to do with feeling and the other with a program. For the present I shall speak only of the feeling. The point of departure is love, the noblest of all human feelings. It was specifically of this that the young lady asked.

There are two places in religious literature where the quotations cited by the lady are most often found—in the Bible and in a large number of forms of the Christian service of Holy Communion, where they are referred to as, "The Summary of the Law." As a first step toward their understanding, it might be well to consider the words in each of these two historic contexts. The biblical passage, from the Gospel of Matthew, starts out with these words. "Then went the Pharisees and took counsel how they might entangle him in his talk." These men, joined later that same day by the Sadducees, were really not interested in learning anything. They were playing games, trying to trick Jesus in his talk. First the Pharisees asked him, "Is it lawful to give tribute to Caesar, or not?" Then the Sadducees had their turn. They took flight into the realms of sheer, ridiculous speculation. Suppose, they said, seven brothers all married the same woman, in each case after she had been widowed, in the hereafter whose wife would she be?

Then the Pharisees moved in again. One of them, a

lawyer, "asked him a question, tempting him, and saying, 'Master, which is the greatest commandment in the law?'" Jesus' answer was immediate. "Thou shalt love the Lord thy God with all thy heart, and with all thy soul, and with all thy mind. This is the first and great commandment. And the second is like unto it, Thou shalt love thy neighbor as thyself. On these two commandments hang all the law and the prophets." Then it was Jesus' turn to ask a question. "What think ye of Christ? Whose son is he?" The water was getting deep, and they all backed away as fast as they could. They were not really seeking to understand, and so they had no more stomach for the discussion.

Here again is emphasized the point made a little earlier: the only proper way to ask serious religious questions is seriously. Today, as of old, the world is full of people who purport to be interested in matters of religion but whose interest is not more than casual curiosity or an attempt to display their own cleverness. They ask questions, having prepared themselves ahead of time to reject all answers. It is well to remember that the immortal words here considered were originally uttered in answer to a question which, if not impertinent in itself, was asked by an impertinent man. He got a better answer than he deserved—not an elaboration but a summary, and a summary not of the whole of the Christian faith but of just one aspect of it. It might also be well to remember that the identity of him who asked the question has long since been lost forever. Even his question is seldom quoted. It is the answer which has endured—and He who gave the answer.

Had that unknown questioner been as serious in his desire to understand as he ought to have been—to have asked such a serious question—he would have followed his first question with another. "How can I so love God?" The point cannot be made too emphatically: unless one has a deep, heart-felt desire for enlightenment, there is no point in proceeding further. The structure of faith in its infancy is too delicate to withstand the ravages of ridicule. In this it is like a newborn child. Eventually it will be strong enough to defend itself—but hardly the first day. For those who are willing to pick up the question in their arms as they would pick up a newborn child, careful to give it the support it needs and still not to smother it, there are rewards. One may harbor doubts, as did the man who said, "Lord, I believe; help Thou mine unbelief." Skepticism and bewilderment are not sins. Cynicism is. To study these words in their original setting does not begin to answer the question, "How can I believe?" But it does suggest the proper atmosphere for the asking, and that is important.

Consider them now in their other most common context. The phrase "the summary of the law" refers to the fact that these words are used in certain services of worship as a substitute for the Ten Commandments, as an actual summary. I believe that this fact provides us with the beginning of an answer to the question, "How can I love God with all my heart and soul and mind?" To love God, as to love a human, means, among other things, to try to please Him. That means to do what He would like us to do. What that is God has made very clear. It means to have no other gods, no graven images, not to take His name in vain, to keep the Sabbath as a holy day, to honor one's father and mother. It also means not to murder, commit adultery, steal, bear false

witness, or covet. Most of us, I fear, will find this an
unsatisfactory answer. What most of us have in mind,
when we think of loving God, with all our heart, and
soul, and mind, is a *feeling*, a warm glow, a thrill, an all-
pervading excitation—the kind of sensation we experienced when we first declared our love to our bride- or
husband-to-be. We think that to fulfill this first commandment we ought to feel in love all the time, every
minute. More about that later.

Meanwhile, let us admit that that is not how it usually is between husbands and wives. The question asked
a bride and groom at the time of their marriage is
almost as demanding as the First Commandment. "Wilt
thou love her, comfort her, honor and keep her, in sickness and in health, and forsaking all others, keep thee
only unto her, so long as ye both shall live?" Most
married people would have to admit that over the
years they have not been able to live up to this very
well. Yet insofar as they have succeeded at all, has it
not been because each has tried to please the other in
as many ways as possible? It is proverbial that doing
dishes and housework and diapers are prosaic mani-
festations of the great declarations of love with which
marriages generally start. But warm glow or no warm
glow, these disagreeable chores are still among the
ways that a woman expresses her love for her husband.
Sometimes the glow is there; sometimes not. Sometimes
there is indifference. Sometimes there are fights. Sometimes unfaithfulness. Still, when the relationship sur-
vives, love—received as well as given—is the ingredient
of survival.

So is it in our love of God. We cannot expect always
to be overcome with emotion. Sometimes the demands

of love may be discouragingly prosaic. To eschew covetousness, for example, is a pretty unromantic way to love God—a little like doing the breakfast dishes. But there can be no escaping the fact: part of the answer to how we can love God with our whole heart and soul and mind is simply to go about doing the things that we know will please Him, however unexciting and lacking in romance they may sometimes be. Sometimes, even, the warm glow of romance comes as a result of such efforts, rather than being the cause— most often, in fact. If it were otherwise, it would not have been necessary for Jesus to start his pronouncement about love with the words, "Thou shalt." There must be discipline, even in love.

To illustrate, I have used the love between humans as an analogy. It is the best we have. But it is more than an analogy. It is a fundamental part of the answer. From the First Commandment Jesus moved immediately to the second which, as he pointed out, is like the first. "Thou shalt love thy neighbor as thyself." I believe that this is more than a corollary to the first. I believe that the two are inextricably bound together, so much so that Jesus felt he had to add the second, although the question asked him had to do only with the first. To love one's neighbor is to love God, very definitely, very clearly, and very precisely.

Generally, we are inclined to think of the Second Commandment as an obligation, a duty that is not always easy to perform, another demand following the stern "Thou shalt." It might be helpful, therefore, to think of this commandment for a moment not as the unpleasant necessity of loving our most unlovable neighbor, but rather as an opportunity to cultivate those relationships we most enjoy. Let us think of those neighbors we have found most winsome, to whom we have been most naturally drawn, whom we have instinctively admired and loved. In my own life I can think of six men in particular who have significantly helped me to love God. Everyone has a similar list. Two of the men in my life happened to be clergymen, two were businessmen, one a teacher, and one a surgeon. None has been a saint, though all have had a fundamentally religious outlook on and interpretation of life. All have had some spiritual qualities, though not always the same ones. Among them is courtesy, humility, and (common to them all) a great love of life. Each in his way and by the example of his own life has suggested to me the thought that if God has made man after His own Image, then God must be something like each of these men. Each has made it easier for me to love God with all my heart and soul and mind—for I have loved them so, and, rightly or wrongly, presumed to count that as loving God.

There is also a seventh person, a man whom I never met, who has been dead for seven hundred years—St. Francis of Assisi. Through the pages of books this man won my heart. His love I found contagious, cutting through mere time as though it were eternity. Imagine a saint with a sense of humor! His simplicity I have found absolutely disarming. Before it even a psychoanalyst would have to succumb. During one of the crusades St. Francis was the only man in the world who thought that the way to end these conflicts was for someone to convert the Sultan to Christianity. So he made the journey, taking his life in his hands, and did his best to persuade the Sultan to change his belief.

He did not succeed, but he so charmed the Sultan that
he thanked St. Francis and let him go his way un-
harmed. To anyone who seriously wants to love God,
I recommend St. Francis, the greatest intermediary the
world has ever known.

The greatest, that is, save one. It was part of the
genius of St. Francis that he learned to love God by
loving his Son. For the Christian, this is the largest and
most important part of the answer to the question of
how to love God. When Jesus finally came to question
the Pharisees and Sadducees, his question, unlike theirs,
was not impertinent. It was pertinent. "What think ye
of Christ? Whose son is he?" No other faith in the history of the world, I believe, offers such a magnificently
precise answer to the question of how to love God. The
best way to love God, and the easiest way, is to love
Jesus Christ. Inevitably some will argue that loving
Christ is just about as hard as loving God. But that is
not true, unless we simply do not know the man, unless
we have never made an effort to become acquainted
with Him. His story is easily available, much more easily
available, indeed, than that of St. Francis. You can find
the account of His life beside your bed in every hotel
room in America. And it is just as much a part of history
as the life of St. Francis. Like all human relationships,
however, time and effort are required to reach understanding. Every friendship has to be nurtured. But the
promise is great. "He that hath seen me hath seen the
Father."

But what of the warm glow mentioned earlier? So
far I have tried to answer the question of how to believe in terms of technique. How, specifically, can I go
about learning to love God? Consciously to follow a

method is part of the answer to another aspect of the word "how"—How can I know the feeling? But there is more to the answer than following a method. I am sure many of us are a little disappointed in God, not just in the way He runs the world but even more in His personal, individual dealings with us. Whatever orthodoxy we possess supplies us with a lot of right answers about God. But they are sterile. Probably they do not please God, and they certainly do not please us. We want more. We long for the sort of religious experience, the warmth and the intimacy, yes, the reality, which has so often been described in holy writ and in the writings of holy men. In a passage which the translators of the New English Bible have entitled "The Calling of a Christian," St. Peter, addressing himself to acknowledged believers, wrote: "Praise be to the God and Father of our Lord Jesus Christ, who in his mercy gave us new birth into a living hope. . . . The inheritance to which we are born is one that nothing can destroy or spoil or wither. . . . You have not seen him, yet you love him; and trusting in him now without seeing him, you are transported with a joy too great for words, while you reap the harvest of your faith. . . ."

That is not our experience. Though we may remember occasional moments of transport in the early history of our faith, we cannot honestly say that the "inheritance to which we are born is one that nothing can destroy or spoil or wither." Wither it has! So that too often in our worship we are either lulled by the beauty of the literature of the service or horrified at our hypocrisy as we repeat words we are not at all sure in our heart of hearts we either understand or believe.

"You must stand in awe of him while you live out

Love

your time on earth," said St. Peter. But we don't. We
are not proud of our failure. We would like, perhaps
more than anything else in the world, to "stand in awe
of him." We just don't and we fear that we never can.
First we blame ourselves. Then at last, like Job, we
blame God. If He cares so much for us, why can't He
make His presence felt more strongly? If He wants us
to love Him, why must He be so nebulous? St. John
said, "He that loveth not his brother whom he hath
seen, how can he love God whom he hath not seen?"
How indeed?

What we long for in our religion (and I believe most
people do long for it, even those not admittedly very
religious) is to be awed, to be moved, to have our
spirits stirred. As I suggested earlier, we want to love
God and we want to *feel* it. We want to be in love with
God, for we know enough to believe that such an experience might be the height of transport. How can we
so love God? As a curse, God is said to have hardened
the heart of Pharaoh. We want to be under no such
curse.

How to experience a feeling of ecstasy in loving God
is a burning question, more so than that implied by the
other interpretation of the word "how." By its nature it
is fraught with emotion. But to find an answer we must,
as before, come down to earth and, as it turns out, on
a spot not too far from where we were before. First
we must recognize that we expect too much, that we
ask too much. The feeling we long for, the awareness
we crave, the sensitivity of spirit we would nurture, is
known to us in a number of the circumstances of ordinary life—at the moment of falling in love; at the first
sight or touch of a newborn son, in the occasional

presence of greatness, in the sudden vision of beauty. But the experience is not something that happens every day. Husbands get used to their wives and wives to their husbands; both can become exasperated with those very children whose first arrival on this earth brought such a thrill. We know from the testimony of others that the constant daily association with greatness lessens the awe. ("A prophet is not without honor *save* in his own home.") The first time I ever saw the Cathedral of Notre Dame in Paris, I was thrilled, as anyone seeing it for the first time would be. Here is indeed a very beautiful thing that man has wrought. The George Washington Bridge, however, has its beauty and grandeur too. But since I see it about a hundred times a year, I cannot expect always to be as moved as I was when I first beheld Notre Dame.

If, during an entire lifetime of association with God, we have never known the thrill of love or life or grandeur or beauty, then something is wrong—not necessarily incurable, but wrong. But surely it is unreasonable to expect to be transported in heart and soul every day. "These are things," said St. Peter, "that *angels* long to see." Such moments must be, ought to be, rare. We have no right to expect more, or to be disappointed when the moment cannot be produced simply at the behest of our own wills, however ardently we yearn.

Still we do yearn, and it is not unreasonable to want to know the feeling at least once in a while. So we stay with the question, How? To say that it cannot happen often is the beginning of an answer, but no more than a beginning. The next step is to be able to know God when we see Him. He is in the husband or wife we love, in the child we love, in the order and beauty of His creation, in the inspiration He gives for the beauty made by man, in man's greatness when he is great. He is Goodness, Beauty, and Truth. He *is* Life. And He *is* Love. Whenever we are transported by any true love we may put it down as loving God; indeed, *must* put it down as loving God.

Of course, if our whole soul has begun to wither, so that nothing in life so moves us, then it is a different matter and a different question—not how can I love God, but how can I love? If there is no spark of faith in anything in life, then the flame of love will not burn. But if the spark is there, it can be fanned into a flame— not easily perhaps but hopefully. And, whenever there is a flame, it need not be a pagan heresy to call it loving God. It is a little like being homesick. When a young man goes off into the service or is away from home for the first time, he feels sharp pangs of longing which he recognizes as homesickness. He is right to consider this feeling an expression of love and to think of it first of all as love for his mother. But it is more than that. It is the refrigerator, the family car, freedom, a chance to sleep late in the morning, his own room, and his own nice, warm bed. But are not all of these a part of what home is all about? And is not his mother largely responsible for them and for the spirit of the place? Is it not proper to count all of his longing as love for her? So, when we love what God has wrought, whether family, friends, creation, or whatever, we are—if we will but acknowledge it—loving God.

All of this, however, is still not quite enough. We would like, I suspect, very specifically to be able to come into a church at a set hour of a Sunday morning and love God and feel it even as we felt it when we took our lover's hand on a moonlit summer's night to make our first declaration. Such a surge of feeling may have happened once or twice in church: when we were confirmed, or stood before the marriage altar, or knelt beside a friend in a moment of great bereavement. Why cannot it happen more often?

I believe it can. We have to work at it, even as we work at the recapture of the moments of first rapture for a mate. How often does a husband say to his wife, "I love you"? And, if often, how many times do the words just slip past his lips, without much thought or feeling? Yet the habit is good—not hypocrisy, but rather a pattern out of which that old feeling will sometimes leap. So too with other habits and customs and cere- monies—an anniversary celebrated, a kiss, a hand held as of old, a look with eyes open not only to see but to show one's own heart. These can be mundane and routine and often will be. But, if they are not aban- doned, they will not always be so.

So may it be as we love God. There must be disci- plines—a strange word in the context of emotion, but paradoxically proper withal—reading, study, ordered thought. (How often has any one of us thought hard about God, for twenty minutes at a time, for example? At best we give Him a fleeting moment of wonder. St. Francis is said once to have repeated these words to himself over and over again for one whole night: "My God and All, what art Thou and what am I?") And there must be worship, corporate and private, free and formal—and regular.

The monastic life, as mentioned earlier, is foreign to most of us and beyond our comprehension. But we cannot brush aside the persistence of its witness through

Love

the centuries, and so some brief consideration of it might here again be profitable. We cannot all be monks and nuns, nor would God have us be. But it has nevertheless been out of such lives of discipline and devotion that have come most of the great moments of religious transport, such as those we long for. How are those moments achieved? If we cannot or will not wholly imitate, we might at least be tutored. Somewhere between the price paid by monks and nuns for loving God and the unbelievably presumptuous demands we place on that one hour we devote to God's love out of a week's one hundred and sixty-eight lies a reasonable ground where we might stand—or kneel—with reasonable expectations.

Even monks are not daily transported by their love of God, I am sure. Once my eleven-year-old daughter and I entered St. Francis' little chapel of San Damiano outside of Assisi. As we knelt to say our prayers I noticed a friar, who seemed to be concentrating so on his devotions that he appeared not to know we were there. Later, as we got up to leave, my daughter inadvertently kicked the kneeling bench, knocking it over with a crash. The friar jumped very nearly out of his skin, and I saw that he had in fact been absolutely sound asleep. Still, I am certain that his way of life leads him to a greater awareness of the love of God than mine and that I could learn much from him.

But "How long, O Lord, how long?" cried Isaiah. And so do we. The fallow days can be discouraging. Still, I believe there is no better way. And perhaps those fallow days are part of love's sacrifice so that, as St. Peter said, "now we smart a little while, if need be, under trials of many kinds." Our impatience to be paid

for our love (we *say* so that we may love some more)
may be such a trial. Is it not a selfish love that would
have its rewards guaranteed in advance? When we cannot love life we must trust it. When we cannot love God
we must trust Him. It happens that the Christian faith
provides for love's failures. They are human, and therefore common to us all. It also makes a promise to those
who persevere. "Humble yourselves then under God's
mighty hand, and He will lift you up in due time."

He does it with His love for us. It is said that we love
God "because He first loved us." Any discussion about
how we can love God, whether it is a matter of technique or of a certain feeling, is bound to be illuminated
by this fact. To have some comprehension of how God
loves us is to understand better than by any other way
how we can love Him, indeed how we can love. How
does God love us?

I would like to begin with a modern parable about
seven people. Five of them have names: Harvey, Grace,
Kenneth, David, and Amy. The other two are nameless. Harvey and Grace are husband and wife. Kenneth
and David are their two sons. Neither Harvey nor Grace
were ever fortunate enough to have had any formal
education beyond the level of high school. Their two
sons, thanks to their own talents and the love of their
parents, have had first-class educations at outstanding
American universities. Kenneth went on to graduate
study in England. While there he met and fell in love
with Amy. She was British, and they planned to be
married in England. They seemed to be as much in
love and as perfectly suited to each other as any two
young people could be.

Naturally Kenneth's mother and father and brother
wanted nothing more on this earth than to be able to

attend the wedding. But there was no money for the trip to England. David, who was still on scholarship in an American university and who had to work in the summers to make ends meet, nevertheless decided that he would find a way. In addition to his regular summer job, he took on extra work at night and on week ends, and with that he figured he could just about make his passage money by the end of August, when the wedding was to take place.

Meanwhile, the two nameless friends, both former teachers of Kenneth and David, decided that Grace should make the trip too and see her eldest son married. Saying nothing to Grace, they each undertook summer tutoring on a back-breaking schedule, made enough money to buy her a plane ticket and gave it to her. So Grace was able to go to her son's wedding.

David began to think. His father really should go in his place. And so one day he drew his father aside and presented him with his ticket. Harvey was completely stunned. To regain his composure he decided to go to the movies that night and think the whole thing over. Though he bought a ticket, he never went inside the theatre. Instead, for three hours he walked the streets. It is more blessed to give than to receive. Finally he came home and decided to accept his second son's offer. So on the appointed day Kenneth and Amy were married in England, and Harvey and Grace were there. David and the two nameless teachers stayed home. This is a parable of love—the love of a young man and a young woman, of a husband and wife, of a mother and father and sons, of brothers and friends and teachers.

It says something about what it means to love. Above all else, to love means to bring forth love. Love begets love, propagates, love, elicits love. This is the meaning of the parable. To say, "God so loved the world" is to say something not only about God but about the state of the world. There *is* love in it, gloriously contagious love, which cannot be stamped out. It is as wholesome and persistent as radioactive fall-out is pernicious. Neither crosses nor persecutions nor indifference have been able to drive it from the earth. The Christian faith teaches its adherents to believe that nothing ever will, not even nuclear explosions. To love means many things, but first of all it means that there is always an answer, an endless echo from the hills. Or was the first cry from the hills and the echo in us? If there is no one to hear, the music of love plays on, until again there is someone, and it swells once more, increasing itself, begetting itself anew. God so loves the world.

To love means other things as well. Another parable. Ruth, a young Moabite woman, lost her husband and out of love attached herself to her mother-in-law. When the mother-in-law felt she must return to her own country, Ruth insisted upon accompanying her. After nearly three thousand years her words are so familiar they need not be repeated—yet so beautiful that they must be. "Whither thou goest, I will go; and where thou lodgest, I will lodge; thy people shall be my people, and thy God my God." So she went with her and joy and beauty followed.

To love means to identify one's self as closely as one can with love's object. It means to hold hands, to get married. It means to find one's self in another, two hearts beating together. One's joy is the other's. One's sorrow is the other's. It means to fear for, to hope for, to care for, to laugh with and cry with. This is how God has loved the world, coming into the world a man, wrestling in the wilderness of his heart with temptation, praying until the sweat broke out on his forehead, deceived by a friend, suffering physical pain and even a moment of despair. God has so loved man that He became a man and dwelt among us. God so loves the world.

But to love means still more. It is not always a natural flow of emotion. It is not always so easy as to *fall* in love. To love means to conquer hate, its bitterest and most formidable foe. The heart is the instrument of love, and sometimes, as I have already suggested, that instrument must be commanded. "I say unto you, love your enemies," is an imperative. Who is my enemy? Khrushchev? Oh, as a matter of principle, I could love him. I'll never have to meet him. But in the immediate and recurrent relationships of daily living, it may not be so easy. There are times when the enemy may be your own wife or your own son or your sister or brother or father or your best friend. Between you and any of them there can be hate. To love means to conquer hate. A Roman soldier, callous enough to have looked on at the crucifixion, perhaps even to have gambled for the victim's clothing, at last looked at Him dead on the cross and said, "Truly, this was the Son of God." God so loves the world.

To love means to revel in what is good and to adorn weakness with grace. Parents love their children not only for their virtues but also for their faults, as do husbands their wives and wives their husbands. A clubfoot or a harelip—a breach of trust or a heartbreaking failure—each in its way is eased and softened by love, just as goodness and beauty are enhanced by it. One of the most beautiful lines from any love song I know is Cole Porter's, "Oh Bill, why can't you behave?" Only love could so combine censure and forgiveness in the very same breath.

By love Jesus transformed the impetuousness and weakness of Peter into the rock on which He built His Church. The vehemence of Peter's triple denial was not promising for the future of Christendom. "He denied before them all, saying, 'I know not what thou sayest.' . . . And again he denied with an oath, 'I do not know the man.' . . . Then began he to curse and to swear, saying, 'I know not the man.' " Then he was reminded that he was loved and "he went out and wept bitterly." God so loves the world.

To love means to annihilate time and space and circumstance. A man who is paralyzed from head to foot, unable to do anything else, can still love—and show that love. A soldier, fighting a war in the Pacific, can love his wife six thousand miles away, at home alone, as though he were standing beside her. St. Francis could love Jesus Christ twelve hundred years after the Crucifixion, and love him with a love that itself still lives seven hundred years after that. An old, old man, at the threshold of death, can look upon a newborn child and love him and see in him a future of hope and salvation, and say, "Lord, now lettest thou thy servant depart in peace, according to thy word: For mine eyes have seen thy salvation, which thou hast prepared before the face of all people; a light to lighten the Gentiles, and the glory of thy people Israel." A strange, mysterious lullaby, in which it almost seems as though it were the child holding the old man in his arms and rocking him to sleep with love's assurance. God so loves the world.

Love

To love means to see things always in the best possible perspective. It means to put first things first, to understand what matters most, indeed to be the key to what matters most, since what matters most is to love. The impracticality of newly-weds is legendary, but the pale practicality of the judgment itself is a symptom of an older love's anemia. Many will recall O. Henry's magnificent short story about the poverty-stricken young lovers. Her beautiful hair, down to her waist, was her pride and joy. But she had no comb. He had a handsome gold watch, but no chain. So at Christmas time he went out and sold his watch and bought her a wonderful comb. And she went out and had her hair cut off and sold it and bought him a watch chain. To love means to know that this story really is not sad.

No more is the story of the woman with the alabaster box of very precious ointment with which she annointed the head of Jesus. "And there were some who had indignation within themselves, and said, 'Why was this waste of the ointment made? For it might have been sold for more than three hundred pence, and have been given to the poor.' And they murmured against her. And Jesus said, 'Let her alone; why trouble ye her? She hath wrought a good work on me. For ye have the poor with you always, and whensoever ye will ye may do them good: but me ye have not always. She hath done what she could.'"

Some time ago there was a particularly sad death in our family, and the neighbors gathered to see what they could do, as neighbors will. An old fellow stopped by who had worked on the place years before, mowing lawns, dumping garbage, and doing other chores. He was not a very bright fellow. I met him in the kitchen and, between his tears and his natural ineptitude with words, he could not speak at all. So he leaned down and picked up the garbage pail and took it out and dumped it as of old. He did what he could, and it was eloquent.

To love means always to do what one can and always to have a sure instinct for what that is. For to love means to listen to love. God so loves the world.

At last, to love means to sacrifice one's self, not bravely, not self-consciously, but gladly and unconsciously, without calculation. To love means finally to escape one's self altogether and to be free, free to rejoice and be exceedingly glad. Think just once again of St. Francis, whose cardinal principles were poverty, chastity, and cheerfulness. Think again of the modern parable of the seven people and the wedding in England. Of course the bride and groom and father and mother rejoiced. But so did David and his friends at home, knowing that their sacrifices for the sake of others were really not sacrifices at all. Because of their love, they were happily—joyously—simply doing what they wanted most to do. God so loves the world having sacrificed Himself for it, not grimly, but "for the joy that was set before him."

Having started with the question, "How can I love the Lord my God with all my heart and all my soul and all my mind?" it seems now that we have come full circle. Our love for God is illuminated by His love for us. But His love for us, it would appear, can best be understood in terms of our own love for whatever is. To be able to believe that whatever exists must be His is to be that much blessed in our love and strengthened in our faith.

Money

"The love of money is the root of all evil things, and there are some who in reaching for it have wandered from the faith and spiked themselves on many thorny griefs." There are few passages of Scripture more familiar to churched and unchurched alike than the first part of that sentence; yet not many maxims are more generally disbelieved. It is a kind of joke, like "Cherchez la femme." It has to be followed quickly by another joke and some nervous laughter, lest one be taken seriously. To the extent that it is believed, it has to do with very rich neighbors, whose lives seem to lack direction, which lack can be safely attributed (if the neighbors are obviously enough richer than we) to "too much money." As for the rest of the world, obviously the root of all evil is not *love* of money but *lack* of money.

Even if one were to take no issue with such a proposition, however, there is one point on which all should agree: money is a problem. And from family financial fights, from suicides at times of national market crises, from individual moral disintegration caused by financial difficulties of one kind or another, it should be obvious that most often money is a *spiritual* problem. At least it gnaws at the spirit, interfering with happiness, threatening love, undermining courage, leaving its mark on mercy, justice, and common decency. Indeed, if there is any real issue to be taken with the Scriptural passage above, it is with the second part, "and there are some who in reaching for it have wandered from the faith and spiked themselves on many thorny griefs." Not "some," but positively millions; not "spiked" merely but impaled.

Looking back over what has already been discussed —Death, Marriage, Children, Moods, Happiness, and Love—one is struck by the thought that money can and very often does have a bearing on each in one way or another. Money occupies the thoughts of many people continually, and to the extent that it becomes an obsession, it leaves its mark—and its mark is a scar. Without bothering to question just yet the proposition that *love* of money is a problem only with the very wealthy and *lack* of money a problem with the rest of the world, let us begin by accepting the fact that money is a problem to almost everyone. Maybe St. Timothy's statement that its love is "the *root* of *all evil things*" is a bit strong, but surely it has caused a lot of trouble. If a man were armed with a faith that could help him cope with this one kind of trouble, he would be well armed.

Nobody should infer from what has been said that money is all evil. It can't be. If it were all bad, it would have no capacity to seduce. Like the Devil himself, it has its attractive side. It has a legitimate function in human society, and often it serves that function most satisfactorily. The familiar phrase "for love or money"

suggests something of what that function is, to moti-
vate; and at first glance one is astonished by what good
company money seems to keep in this regard. The implication of "for love or money" is that these are the
two most effective sources of motivation, and so they
may well be. There are others—a sense of duty, fear,
lust for power, et cetera. But it is evident that in the
day-by-day operations of humans living together most
of what is done—the things that need and ought to be
done, as well as some others—are done either out of
love or for pay.

Nor of the two is money always such a poor and
ignoble second. The words "amateur" and "professional," as they are used in the world of sports and in
other areas of American life in their almost complete
and ironic reversal of meaning reflect some significant
changes in attitudes. The word "amateur" still suggests
one who performs for love, but often it also connotes
one who performs not very well—a *rank* amateur, we
say. A professional is still one who performs out of a
sense of commitment to a particular area of performance and who therefore gets paid. (Since he has made
it his full time occupation, he has to get paid.) But the
word also suggests someone who performs skillfully and
with precision. So at least in some areas of life, it would
seem that money is actually a stronger motivating force
than love.

In the world of American sports the issue is marvel-
ously confused, since some amateurs get paid and some
professionals love their work. But you can still tell the
two apart. Almost always the professionals are more
proficient. And the reason why amateurs sometimes get
paid (whether under or over the table doesn't matter)

is because love, as a motivating force, sometimes proves insufficient. Hence the tennis bum, who, as an amateur, won't play without some pay and who turns professional as soon as he is good enough to ask for more pay, discovers to his amazement that as a pro, he isn't a bum any more.

That money is a powerful and effective motivator can be demonstrated in almost any kind of activity. Try, for example, to get your teen-age son to do chores around the house—for love. Then let your next-door neighbor hire him for pay and compare your own observations of your son's attitude and performance with your neighbor's report. It couldn't be the same boy! Anyone who has had experience with volunteer workers in churches and schools and service organizations knows how exasperating it can be to try to get amateurs to do anything right and on time. Happily, it is not always so, and when it is otherwise it is thoroughly otherwise. I am not suggesting that love is not good as a motivating force. At its best it is the best. But when there is not enough love, money can be a very effective substitute— and a clean and honorable one as well.

One might think that in an organization like the Red Cross, for example, the volunteers—just because they are volunteers—would be specially honored and that the paid worker would be somewhat looked down upon as a hired hand in an area where love should rule and nobody should be so crass as to accept money for his work. But in fact it is often otherwise. The paid worker is looked upon as a professional, that is, dependable, trained, efficient. He is respected as such, and relied upon as such, and usually performs as such—with both skill and devotion. And finally, to carry the point to the ultimate in irony, what is it that has kept the so-called oldest profession in the world going all these centuries? Is it not that men have sometimes found that the love they could not get for love they could get for money? There are accounts in literature, presumably reflecting the realities life, of men who have paid prostitutes not for any physical satisfactions at all but just for companionship and friendly talk. *Financially,* such an arrangement might occasionally be more satisfactory than marriage. Of course it is always wrong, never right. But such buying and selling of affection is certainly strong and persistent and ancient testimony suggesting that perhaps money does belong with love as a high motive for humanity. Never its equal, but not always such a bad substitute. Like love, money can be corrupted and it can be corrupting. But perhaps one should wait until it has become so before one condemns it out of hand.

The paramount question, then, is corruption. Where there is corruption, there is evil, because corruption is evil, and it does not matter very much what is corrupted. One reason why the volunteer worker is often inferior to the professional is that he is sometimes inclined to think of himself as the very personification of good will. So he may be tempted to cut corners here and there, apparently with the thought, "Since what I have to offer is good will, freely given, you have no hold on me. Of course I'll do the best I can, but I'm not punching any time clocks. Whatever you get from me is a gain, so just be thankful." This is a corruption of love and, of course, can be far worse than the corruption of money. In contrast, the professional attitude (a phrase which has come into common use by no accident) is

cleaner and more wholesome and even more altruistic.
No wonder the words "amateur" and "professional"
tend sometimes to have taken on overtones of lukewarm
ineptitude as against well-intended competence, even
though in origin neither word implied either meaning.

But what about the corruption of and by money? Let
me begin with an example that is very familiar to me.
In a small independent school, the headmaster gets
involved in a little bit of everything. Over the years I
have had occasion to talk about family finances with
hundreds of parents who want scholarships for their
sons. And as a fund raiser I have talked with other
hundreds of people (sometimes even the same ones)
about gifts, tax deductions, and all the rest that goes
with that weird operation. There are enough exceptions to prove the rule and to give one heart, but there
can be no denying the weight of evidence that most
people are far from their best when they are talking
about or spending or gathering or counting or thinking
about money. It is astonishing how open and above-
board and outgoing and easy and relaxed certain people can be on every subject in the world—except money.
But mention money and you can see on their faces a
sudden, distorting change. They become evasive. They
give every evidence that there just is not anything that
is more personal, more intimate, and less anyone else's
business than their own financial affairs. Such reticence
might be acceptable if these people felt the same way
about a lot of other personal matters and defended their
privacy in other areas with the same aggressiveness.
Ask a man about his religious or political beliefs, and
he may be embarrassed and hesitant to speak of them.
Nevertheless the chances are that even if he is a little

shy he'll make a stab at it. But ask him what his salary is, and he'll be insulted and indignant and figuratively throw you out of the house. In some sections of suburbia (such a favorite target for moralizing, now that everyone seems to have lost interest in the farmer's daughter and the traveling salesman) adultery is frankly accepted as something to condone, forgive, and wink at—at least in comparison to cheating with money. If it gets about town that a man is too interested in another man's wife, eyebrows are raised, sotto voce comments made, but nothing is done. If it is discovered that a man has mishandled money, however, or that he has run up debts recklessly, then the community moves against him. The rules about money are sacred. To break them is unforgivable.

Money corrupts in many ways. It undermines forgiveness and compassion and in the process warps and twists a man's whole attitude toward his fellow man. It starts early. In a boys' boarding school or residential college, one of the few unforgivable sins is stealing money. This thing, which was created by society as nothing more or less than a convenience for barter and service, which at its best can perform in man's best interests in a very worthy fashion, suddenly becomes the touchstone of morality, the frame of reference, the basis for perspective. And money has no morality; it has no power to refer to anything but itself; and it has nothing whatever to do with vision. What sadder thing could be said about American morality than that we have tried to reduce value and worth to the measure of dollars?

And money corrupts by undermining generosity. I once had several sessions in my office with a man whose son had some serious problems. I shall never forget the face of that man as we talked on those occasions. It was full of a mixture of hope and anxiety and desperate fear —much more fear than the situation called for, it seemed to me. Nevertheless, I found his apprehension and his helplessness attractive. His concern was a reflection of his love for his son, among other things. Happily his son's problems in time were resolved. Some years later, under very different circumstances, I called on that same man in his office to ask him for financial help for our school. Now he was in the driver's seat— and the driver's seat was grimly symbolic. It was a tight swivel chair, pulled close to an old-fashioned roll-top desk. The ticker was running and it was so arranged that the tape moved directly across the man's lap, like a seat belt. As a further precaution he held it in both hands. As he listened to my story, I could hardly recognize the man I had known before. He was the picture of a medieval miser—his mouth distorted and his eyes, when not fixed on me, darting left and right, studying his seat belt. We were talking about money now. And he was not about to let go—of anything.

Money also corrupts by seduction. I have said that it can and does provide an effective and not immoral motivation for constructive human action. But it can also seduce. If there is one area where I think large corporation may be charged with immorality, it is in the way they use financial incentive. Of course the greed and the innocence (if one can imagine them as walking hand in hand) of the individual employee plays its part. Still—unconscionably, it seems to me—large-scale employers are guilty of getting the best years of men's lives on the promise of more and more money, knowing

that only rarely will that promise be fulfilled, and knowing also that when it is not, the disillusionment will
often be devastating. What is still worse, even when
the promise *is* fulfilled, the disillusionment may prove
just as shattering. Like a carrot on a stick, money leads
many a man down a path toward his own destruction.
It is sad, but not a year passes that one or more men in
their forties do not come to me asking for jobs as teachers. Until then they have spent their lives chasing
money. Some have caught it and some have not, but in
either case there is a hollowness. Their eagerness to
find something of lasting value to fill their lives is sad—
sad because usually it is too late.

Jesus said, "Ye cannot serve God and mammon."
The new English translation is more direct. "No servant
can be slave to two masters; for either he will hate the
first and love the second, or he will be devoted to the
first and think nothing of the second. *You cannot serve
God and Money.*" Does this mean that the answer to
this problem for the religious man is that he may not
touch money, may have nothing to do with it? Must he
pledge himself to poverty? There is a persistent strain
of Christian thought that does say just that. There is
not a single monastic order that does not have poverty
as one of its vows, such is the solemnity with which a
vast number of believers for a very large number of
centuries have taken the words of St. Timothy: "The
love of money is the root of all evil things." But I do
not believe the interpretation needs to be that extreme.
St. Timothy spoke of the *love* of money, and Jesus spoke
of *serving* money. When money masquerades as love,
it is a sorceress; when it poses as God, it is the Devil.
What we all need to learn from the monastics is not

that it is impossible to live with the fact of money without being corrupted, but that it is so difficult that we must be more wary than most of us have ever thought we needed to be.

In my fiscal innocence, I confess I was shocked to read the following in the November 29, 1963 issue of TIME magazine, the first issue to come out after the assassination of President Kennedy: "It was the wildest performance in years on the floor of the New York Stock Exchange. Caught at their favorite luncheon spots when the news of President Kennedy's assassination reached them at 1:40 P.M., many Wall Streeters left their meals and rushed back through the streets to find the market already besieged with sell orders. Ignoring the firm rule that prohibits running on the exchange floor, traders ran about frantically, bowling each other over in their haste. By the time the board of governors announced the closing of the exchange at 2:07 P.M. . . . the Dow-Jones industrial average had plummeted 21.16 points, running up losses of $11 billion." At 2:07 P.M. on that awful day in American history, the news of the President's death was 27 minutes old on Wall Street. It is distressing to think of the number of Americans with hearts in their pocketbooks that it must have taken to create that kind of chaos. That shameful performance pumps new life into some rather time- and shop-worn words, "Where your treasure is there will your heart be also."

Nor was the guilt limited to the "rich." Indeed one well–to–do man, quoted in an article in the New York *Herald Tribune* of November 25th, revealed a deeper sensibility than many investors exhibited. " 'I sat in the board room Friday,' he said, 'and I was appalled at what I saw. I heard one individual tell his man, "Sell me out at any price," and I winced. What happens to people?' " The answer to that question is simply that it depends on where their hearts are. The "individual" in question did not really have to place an order to be sold out at any price. He did not even need a broker. He had sold himself out long before.

In that same article in the *Herald Tribune,* another quotation seems particularly pertinent to this discussion. " 'I can't think of a single company that would be affected by what's happened,' said one investment counselor, a view echoed in other quarters as well. 'No one man is irreplaceable. Maybe there'll be some temporary turmoil. But no company should realistically be affected by President Kennedy's death.' " In its context, I like that statement. It is honest, and straightforward, and very probably true. But since that statement bears the date line of November 25, 1963, the whole context is out of context. Unquestionably the author would himself be horrified to have it quoted at all. Surely he would not want that to be all he had to say about the assassination of the President of the United States. He was speaking, I am sure he would contend, strictly as a financial man. But no man is "strictly a financial man," for, if he is, he is not a man at all but a demon. Money, in itself, is no more evil than sex. But it has the same power to get a lot of people in a lot of trouble, to make them demons.

Financially there are three general divisions of men —the very rich and the very poor and those in between. Because they are fewest in number and most conspicuous (and because none of us is without jealousy) it is most fun to attack the very rich. It was a very rich young man who once asked Jesus, "What must I do to inherit eternal life?" Jesus told him, and the young man was able to give an extremely good account of himself, better, indeed, than most of us could. He had kept all the commandments and furthermore realized that in doing so he had not done enough. "Where do I still fall short?" he asked. "If you wish to go the whole way," said Jesus, "go sell your possessions, and give to the poor, and then you will have riches in heaven; and come and follow me." After hearing these words, continues the story, "he went away with a heavy heart; for he was a man of great wealth." As it stands this story seems to me to focus undue attention on the fact of the man's wealth. It would seem to me that one would not need to be a man of great wealth to go away with a heavy heart after hearing such words. Only a few in Christian history have come anywhere near meeting the challenge of Jesus' words at that moment.

Still, He pressed the point of wealth as a central factor in the situation, and said to his disciples, after the rich young man had walked away, "I tell you this: a rich man will find it hard to enter the kingdom of Heaven. I repeat, it is easier for a camel to pass through the eye of a needle than for a rich man to enter the kingdom of God." In our own bewilderment, we may all take some comfort in the words which immediately follow. "The disciples were amazed to hear this." So are we, even though we have heard it before and the disciples had not.

In theory certain things are obvious about great wealth and its effects upon a man's soul. How is it possible to acquire or to maintain great wealth without exploiting one's fellow man or without being insensitive to the needs of others? It seems to me almost inevitably true that, where there is great wealth, there must have been, somewhere, sometime, either ruthlessness or selfishness or both. But the degree to which one is in a position to condemn others depends upon one's own ruthfulness and one's own generosity. The disciples themselves were more than a little nervous about Jesus' meaning and presumably in consternation asked the question, "Then who can be saved?" Who indeed, for surely the wealthy do not have a corner either on ruthlessness or on selfishness. Jesus' answer, "For men this is impossible; but everything is possible for God," tends to take the poor rich man off the hook for the moment, or rather to throw all the rest of us in with him. One wonders, as a matter of fact, if Jesus' attack on this particular rich man (who did seem rather nicer than most) was not purposely intended to be only an opening wedge into the hearts and consciences of all mankind.

In any case, I think it is high time for people to begin to realize that the corrupting power of money is not dependent upon quantity. Rich people are corrupted by money; and so are poor people; and so is everyone in between, each in his own way. Sin is sin and spiritually there is little difference between the sinful passion with which one person hoards the money he already has and the sinful passion with which another longs for the money he does not have. I do not really believe that the love of money is at the root of *all* evil things, but I do believe it is at the root of a great many. And since you do not have to *have* money in order to *love* money, no one is excluded.

So the question is still "Then who can be saved?"

Money

Without God's help, as Jesus said, no one. But within the framework of the human scheme of things, there is a hint a little more direct and unavoidable than the words about rich men and camels and eyes of needles. The ancient and familiar words from St. Matthew's version of the Sermon on the Mount are, "Blessed are the poor in spirit: for theirs is the kingdom of heaven." Less familiar are the words from St. Luke's version, "Blessed are ye poor: for yours is the kingdom of God." Most modern scholars seem to think that what Jesus actually said was, "Blessed are the poor." Whichever version is the true one, the controversy itself leads us to ask whether poverty in itself is a means of grace. To put it more bluntly: on the whole, are poor people spiritually and morally better than others? On the surface, this doesn't look like the kind of generality that can be argued with profit. Some will even find it offensive. Yet I feel that the question is one which every man ought to ask himself, for the answer, whatever it may be, is important.

I personally think that Jesus did mean to say that poverty in itself is a means of grace, and I take the stand that the proposition is supportable, in theory and in practice. In the first place, suffering is concomitant with virtue. Anyone who has not suffered cannot possibly have reached the heights of virtue, for to exclude suffering is to exclude courage, full sympathy, and even love. To some extent, obviously, poverty involves suffering. So it is a proving ground for courage, a bond of sympathy, and an invitation to love. There are a thousand causes for suffering, of course, but poverty is probably the most nearly universal of all.

Cruel as it often is, poverty is a link which joins man

to his fellow man. Sharing this adversity helps to fan the flames of brotherhood. "God must have loved the poor," Lincoln is supposed to have said, "since he made so many of them." Most of the world is poor. While poverty itself is surely not a virtue, it can be made to grace other virtues. Generosity, for example, will forever be most perfectly portrayed by the widow and her mite. But the elder John D. Rockefeller bestowing his thin dimes was a pitiful and pathetic caricature of generosity. The great foundation since established in his family's name is a nobler effort, serving the community and mankind in scores of ways. But public service is not personal generosity, and in idle moments I sometimes imagine two arrivals at the Gates of Heaven. One is the founder of a great foundation. Under his arm he carries a massive report of the vast number of admirable programs and projects the foundation has supported. The other arrival is a woman. She says simply, "I am the widow."

I confess that I have argued this point—that the poor have a moral and spiritual advantage—with schoolboys for years without notable success. The only concrete illustration I have ever been able to use that has struck any kind of spark with the boys is their experience in hitchhiking. "What kinds of cars usually stop to give you a lift?" Since most of them are accomplished hitchhikers in their spare time, they know the answer. "Not many Cadillacs."

I do not mean to ignore the fact that it is in areas of crowded poverty that one finds a concentration of immorality and crime. But the many who labor that point too often ignore the equally valid point that I would make to them. A half million people live in Harlem.

Money

There is a lot of immorality and crime. But there is also a lot of courage and grace, more, perhaps, than on Park Avenue, *below* 95th Street.

Recently I have had the privilege of living for a year in a very small, poor village in the southern part of France. Poverty is not extreme there—not an actual threat to survival. But nobody has any money; nobody owns anything he does not need; nobody has any margin; and for everybody the struggle is close to desperate. Only sixty people live in the village. One is the postman and one is the mayor and one is the garbage man and one is the garage mechanic and two are school teachers and two run a little store and one is a baker and the rest work in a limestone quarry or are wives or children. All of them work part time in the fields. There is almost no money in the village. People barter for many of the necessities; and they help anyone who needs help. They have sympathy for others and they work hard—always they work hard. They learn to economize and to help each other economize. If a woman has something to bake and no oven—and most people in the village do not have ovens—she takes it to the baker and he lets her put it in his oven while he is baking his bread. When he fixes a neighbor's car, the garage man tries to make it run as well as he can for as little as he can and gets his neighbor involved in the purchase of new parts as seldom as he can. But what is most impressive is the things that these people do without. This dimension of poverty—the constant necessity to make choices—forces them, whether they know it or not, to make moral judgments. What really is first in importance to a man and to his family? What matters most? It is heartening that generosity is usually considered one of the essentials, like food, that cannot be eliminated.

This little village is no kingdom of heaven. It, too, has its sinners. There are gossips and rivalries and some pettiness. At the same time this village is obviously less corrupted by money than many other places in the world. The scarcity does not eliminate corruption, but it does eliminate one major cause of corruption. And that helps. "Blessed are the poor" is a generality and anyone can point to exceptions. But surely the suffering that goes with being poor and the sense of brotherhood which it tends to engender must help to make some people morally and spiritually sturdier.

In times of catastrophe rich and poor alike can rise to great heights of spiritual grace. But among the poor, everyday living is a kind of constant catastrophe, and, to make it otherwise, I believe, the victims of poverty tend to rise to such heights a little more often.

Now who can be saved? Only the poor? And only some of them? I hope not, and I think not. I do not really believe, St. Timothy to the contrary, that Jesus meant to say that money—the lack or love of it—was so crucial to salvation. I do believe that the more money one has the more he has to answer for, in the light of the needs—often the desperate needs—of others. But there are other factors that make up the moral and spiritual pattern of a man's life. And, if money can be kept in its proper place, as a thing, an instrument, a device, it can be a measure of these other factors—not a contributing factor but a measure. It does make a difference what you do with money and how you think about it and how free you can keep yourself from its grip.

Money

My father-in-law had a most wonderful attitude toward money. He thought it was for spending. It didn't matter much to him whether it was his money or someone else's. And strangely enough the someone else's never minded either, largely, I think, because he could make money sing. He had a Robin Hood reputation for being able to "get money out of" rich people and spread it around among the poor and the distressed. But that reputation was very misleading, for Robin Hood stole the money and this man just gathered it. He got it because he had the simple (yet rare) ability to use it in such a way that everyone enjoyed it. Those who gave were made really to *love* to give. And those who received were always helped with such imagination and tact and sheer fun that the help that was given never seemed to be charity. It was pennies from heaven.

For my father-in-law, money was always an incidental element in a human situation. He started with a human need—almost always something not obvious to the rest of the world. This must be done for that man, that needs to be done for such and such an institution. Then it was a game to get the job done, a game in which all could join the fun. Naturally, my father-in-law had the most fun of all. Like anyone else he often worried about not having enough money. But he neither loved it nor scorned it nor was afraid of it. He just laughed at it.

What saved him from its contamination—as much as any of us can be saved—was that he was always primarily concerned with something else. One almost could have said that in his budget *all* expenses were incidental expenses, because money itself was so incidental to all the good he did in his life. He hated fund-raising campaigns, probably because almost all such campaigns—no matter how much they are focused on the new construction or the new endowment—end up counting money in public and measuring success in dollars. All too often the good that is to be accomplished is lost in the souped-up enthusiasm for the means of doing it. My father-in-law, on the other hand, liked to go around simply doing good, confident that when the time came he could somehow find a way. With him, it was truly a matter of faith—faith in people and faith in what is right and faith in what ought to be and a faith in God. The simplicity of that faith was disguised by his own sophistication and given strength by his deep and genuine devotion. Nevertheless, faith was at the root of his life.

As I have already said, I have had a great deal of occasion to confer with a great many people about their family finances in connection with scholarships for their boys. The process is revealing and, for the most part, heartening. It is surprising how many people do not have much money, not from lack of work or talent or ambition but simply because they value other things more highly. Still, or perhaps therefore, these people are capable of making rather unbelievable sacrifices for something which they think is truly important—for example, the education of a son. I am frequently asked—particularly by the more well-to-do, some of whom can be very cynical about the poverty of others—I am asked the question, "Do you really think most people tell you the truth on these scholarship forms?" I am offended, for most do tell the truth, willingly and graciously. And most of them have a much clearer view of the relative importance of things than some of their more wealthy neighbors. But it is not the amount of money that makes the difference. It is the faith. One family will serve to illustrate the point. It is a family which, by American independent school standards, is truly poverty-stricken. They do not have enough clothes; they drive a truly antique car, a desperate necessity for getting both husband and wife to work; and they own absolutely nothing that anyone from any walk of life could call a luxury—except, perhaps, a place for their son in an independent school. Of course the boy has a very large scholarship. A year or so ago the wife's father died and left them his total inheritance, the only one they could ever hope to receive from any source. It was a $500 war bond. Shortly thereafter I received a letter from the family, with the bond enclosed. The circumstances were explained and the letter went on to say, "We had a family meeting and tried to decide what the most pressing need of the family is just now and for the foreseeable future. We decided that it is to express our gratitude to your school. We all agree, not only the son who is with you but his younger brother, who will never be able to attend your school, as well." I happen to know that this is an exceptionally devout family and that the decision must have been reached in a very old-fashioned way, after some family prayers. Maybe it was not the right decision. And surely less faithful people are also capable of arriving at similar heights of generosity. But I cannot escape the thought that such things *usually* happen in the kind of an atmosphere that exists in that family, that such grace is *usually* born out of faith.

In speaking of money in connection with the efficacy of belief, I realize that in the minds of many the relationship between the two is obscure, and unfortunately with reason. It seems to me that the confusion arises largely from the difference between what the Church says about money and what God says about money. While I firmly believe that the Church must be one of our primary sources of knowledge and inspiration about God, I am afraid that what it has said and done about money has seldom been to its credit. This is not to say that I agree with those who constantly carp at the Church for talking about money. It does need money, and usually its needs are more worthy than those of most other institutions; the Church won't get money without asking for it. Still, I confess that the Church often seems to be too much bitten by the modern American craze for drives and buildings and campaigns and special funds. In this it has often hopped on the bandwagon, and the bandwagon is an inappropriate place to find the Church. Too often clergymen are considered capable because of their success in raising money rather than because of their spiritual leadership, which is their appointed task. And vestrymen are selected for the same sort of talents. Whole parishes are deemed successful and alive because of the impressive sums of money raised and spent and displayed. So it is no wonder that some skeptics may be unmoved by the proposition that the Christian faith has anything of particular value to say on the subject of money. Of parishes and of whole denominations, as well as of individuals, it might be said, "Blessed are ye poor: for yours is the kingdom of God."

But to criticize the Church in this regard is not to condemn it wholly, nor does it mean that true faith therefore is necessarily misleading or impotent. It shines brilliantly in many an individual member. If the Church is a primary instrument for the dissemination of God's word, then through it, however indistinctly it may sometimes mutter, that word shall be heard by those with ears to hear. So on the subject of money, as on so many others, I say again that those whose hearts have been touched by faith cope better—no matter how much or how little money they may have—than those whose hearts have not so been touched. If among the blessed the poor are more blessed than the rich, it is not because they have less money but because, having less money, it is likely that their faith is better placed.

Through whatever confusion the Church may have created, the word of God on the subject of money is nevertheless unmistakable. Through His Son, God said, "You cannot serve God and Money." Whatever else that may mean it certainly means that the two are separate. And anything that is separate from God is not of God, and so much the worse for it. Again through His son God said the same thing in a different way. "Pay Caesar what is due to Caesar, and pay God what is due to God." The Roman state under which the people to whom He spoke lived was something less than the kingdom of Heaven. Nevertheless, Jesus recognized that those people had to live in that world; and I think He would recognize our need to live in our world. We too are under the necessity of giving Caesar his due. If only we could see that it is also necessary for us to give God His due, and that this is as practical a necessity as the other. For our salvation, not only in the world to come but in this world, is a practical matter.

Undoubtedly there is a conflict implicit in the Christian concept of faith and money. And it is fundamental.

Money

Nevertheless, it is more paralyzing in theory than in everyday living. A man of good conscience, ever tutored and kept young by his faith, can have a great deal of casual truck with money without his soul being seared beyond redemption. There will be times when he will have to make a real choice between the Almighty God and the almighty dollar. For these moments of decision he will have to be on his guard lest he miss them; and when he faces them, his faith will be put to the test. But without faith he hasn't got a chance.

Faith is the instrument by which a man may best measure the relative importance of things, may know how to put first things first. When it comes to money, there is nothing which it is more important to know. Seen through faith's eyes on its own merits, money is *just never first.*

Courage

There has been no age in the history of man which has not demanded courage, nor any individual human life which has not felt the need for it. Fearlessness, a natural gift possessed by few, if truly by any, is not the same thing. Though fearlessness may be envied in another, like health or wealth or good looks, it is not in itself admirable. Courage, on the other hand, is the weapon by which a man struggles with fear. Courage *is* admirable to the extent that, as a weapon, it is wielded successfully. In action the two often look so much alike that the virtue, courage, is often confused with the talent, fearlessness. As with so many other virtues and talents, men are inclined to attribute the virtue to themselves and the talent to others—a division which somehow seems to relieve the conscience. But when he searches his heart with care, every man knows the difference and is deceived only as he wishes to be deceived.

There is another kind of fearlessness which is like the first only in name. The final fruit and perfect prize of courage, it is a part of the "peace of God which passeth all understanding." Fearlessness of this sort is the calm after the storm and is so far removed from what people mean when they say, "He doesn't know the meaning of the word 'fear,'" that it is a pity that the same word has to be used for both. If there really is a kind of fearlessness which does not know the meaning of the word "fear," it is nothing that can be profitably discussed here. It is important, however, to make the distinction between courage and fearlessness, for courage cannot be understood properly unless one realizes that it starts with the presence of fear, not the absence of it. As a matter of fact, only rarely is fear ever wholly eliminated and then only when one is blessed by a conviction strong enough to keep courage high in the face of no matter what.

Most men are surrounded most of the time by fears which gnaw painfully at their souls. To relieve that pain they must take courage or else cringe and continue to suffer. At first, nearly everyone tries to escape fear by cringing and accepting the pain. Just when a person decides to try courage depends not so much on the intensity of the pain, but rather on the strength of the convictions out of which his courage is born. (Through lack of courage men have been known to suffer an unbelievable amount of pain for incredible lengths of time, needlessly.) At the first sign of a toothache, for example, we suffer in silence, hoping it will go away— obviously the easiest way out. Maybe it is only our imagination, after all. But the ache persists. There is no doubt about the pain; but perhaps it is just some sort of spasm. So we fight off the truth and suffer because we are afraid that if we go to the dentist he will hurt us.

Courage

How long we wait, and how much pain we endure before we go and open our mouths voluntarily and let the dentist do his work will depend primarily not on how desperate is the suffering but rather on our degree of faith in dentistry and the dentist. If our faith is great, we will go soon; if not, we will delay. The courage to act grows out of our belief that what we are doing is the right and efficacious and (we say) "sensible" thing to do. Such, always, is the process of mustering courage. Anyone can do it and everyone has. A courageous man is merely one who does it more often or more impressively or sooner than the rest of us.

In our generation, as in every other, there is a daily need for courage. In fact, it seems to me that there is need for two kinds: the courage to bear and the courage to dare. The former is most common, for the necessity to endure adversity is thrust upon us. For all the marvelous advances that have made it possible for medicine not only to prolong life and maintain good health, but also to relieve suffering, most people still have to cope with acute physical pain at some time or other in their lives. Indeed, it almost seems that the blessings science gives with one hand it takes away with the other. In the world of medicine there is morphine and in the world of mechanics there is the automobile. The two are linked in my mind because, in the college infirmary many years ago, I listened through one whole interminable night to a classmate in the next bed moaning in agony. He was the victim of an automobile accident and he died in the morning. If on the average we suffer less physically than did our ancestors, then we are less prepared for it as well. We are softer, so our need for courage is great. We do not know when we shall have to call upon our store of courage, but we can be sure that sooner or later we will need it.

Physical pain, however, is not the only kind that is thrust upon us to be borne, bravely or not. There are countless situations in daily life which require great courage. Most obvious, of course, is death, not only our own but perhaps even more that of a person close to us. Being older and being a man, I have always gone along gaily on the assumption, expressed openly (and frivolously) many times, that I would die before my wife. Then suddenly one day it occurred to me that in spite of the actuarial figures, she *might* die before me. I was truly paralyzed with fear at the thought that, after all, *I* might have to be the one to carry on year after year alone. Only then did I realize that if her death were so fearful to me, must not mine be so to her? It is not a joking matter. It is fearful. If there is to be any serenity in life, then the contemplation of death—others' perhaps even more than one's own—must be accompanied by courage.

In the same way courage is needed with marriage, in a thousand ways, a thousand times a year; and perhaps two or three times a lifetime in the face of very major crises. So too with the raising of children, very much so. Children can and do inflict pain, pain which cannot always—or ever?—be exorcised by punishment. Sometimes there is nothing to do but endure, bravely if possible. If there is any such thing as happiness for man on earth, it can only be for the courageous. A brave man may often be miserable, but a coward is always so, a vital point that shall be discussed a bit later. As for love and money, they too lead us down paths of pain where courage is called for.

Courage

Courage is such an ancient virtue that we tend to associate it with bygone days, even primitive times. That is a mistake. As a human need and as a spiritual fact, courage changes little from age to age. Thoreau said, "The mass of men lead lives of quiet desperation." He may have been right, but it seems to me that he gave too many men too little credit. There are quite a few who lead lives of quiet courage. Surely the world would be a better place if all men did.

The need for the courage to bear is endless, I think. Some may ask why? True, they say, all men are faced again and again with fearful things thrust upon them which they must bear, but what difference does courage make? If what has to be borne has to be borne, how can you say a man is brave to bear it? And if he is, what of it?

First of all, courage is a matter of grace. It has characteristics we seldom consider. It is, for example, neighborly. It is considerate. It is courteous. And it is a rather glorious expression of love.

My father was one of the most courageous men I ever knew. Before 1929 he had a reasonably successful career in Wall Street, making a little more than his share of money and holding positions of dignity and service to his fellow men. He was not a gambler so he lost nothing in the crash, but the debacle did coincide with long and expensive illnesses of his wife and then of his sister. Both ended in death. By 1933 he had no money and no job. He had remarried and fortunately his new wife was a schoolteacher, for it turned out that her salary was absolutely the only income they had. (She, too, had courage.) For *five* years my father read want ads every morning and walked the streets every

Courage

day looking for jobs. He accepted any work he could get no matter how humiliating it might have seemed to others. For a time he even took a job as a delivery "boy," about which, incidentally, he wrote a quite marvelous little story—in praise of his co-workers. In all those years, never once did he complain; never once did he bemoan his fate; never once did he show even a slight sign of being any less in love with life. His good cheer, which had always been his special hallmark, seemed to his friends and family wholly unmarked and intact. His courage was, I think, a memorable experience for everyone who knew him. It was a thing of many parts. It was neighborly. It was considerate. It was courteous. It was a glorious expression of his love. It was a matter of grace.

Furthermore, it was efficacious for him. His courage did not *hide* his bitterness; it banished it from his heart, kept it from ever entering or even getting its foot in the door. If my father was a happy man—and I think he was, more so than most—then his happiness was largely if not wholly the product of his courage to bear, a courage so great that it was glorious rather than merely grim. Measured as the world so often measures achievement, his life was not much of a success. He must certainly have felt the frustration of defeat during his life, starting with his flunking out of college, continuing through one unhappy marriage and another ending in death, and enduring financial difficulties for the final twenty-five years of his life. Yet I never knew anyone who loved life more or who seemed to have less to complain about. His courage was his secret, and the other qualities—especially humor—which flowed from it. (Are there any virtues or amenities that are not served by courage? Though it is not the source, courage makes room in the soul for generosity and charity and humility and humor and good cheer, as well as honesty and loyalty and all the rest.)

Perhaps I should apologize for speaking so freely about one so close to me. My defense is this: the courage of which I speak is such a very intimate thing that it seemed natural to illustrate it intimately. If, as he reads, anyone feels that his own father or friend might have been as good an example, I am glad. This I take as evidence that there is more courage in the world around us than we sometimes have eyes to see.

One more short word about my father. To confess that his faith was something less than orthodox and that his church attendance was not very regular—except now and then to hear one of his sons preach or the other two sing in the choir—might seem to contradict much that I have said about belief. I think not, for there is no doubt in my mind that my father's courage was born of his faith. One of his very favorite expressions was, "Great Bountiful Jehovah!" And he meant it. He believed in Jehovah and he believed in His Bounty, even though some might say that he himself had not received very much of it. My father believed, and he was better for it.

So far I have spoken only of the courage to bear. The second kind of courage, the courage to dare, is more rare and perhaps more needed on this earth. It is the courage to ask for trouble when the situation demands such action. It is the stuff from which personal morality and public responsibility are made.

The story of Nazi Germany is perhaps a good place to begin a discussion of the courage to dare. The Nazi regime is far enough in the past to be looked at, not with detachment surely, but with some small degree of perspective, even though that perspective is nothing more than our being able to say, "It wasn't us and it isn't today."

In William Shirer's *The Rise And Fall Of The Third Reich* there are two sentences which are haunting. When apparently innocent Germans—decent people who did not beat their wives and children, who went to church on Sundays, obeyed the law and were relatively agreeable to their neighbors—when these people were asked, years after Hitler was dead, how the horror ever developed and how they themselves could have let it come to pass, they almost all replied, according to Mr. Shirer, "We were helpless. There was nothing we could do." To me the most frightening thing about this chapter in world history is not so much the extent of the atrocity as the relative decency of the society out of which it was born. The German people were not barbarians. They had the faults and virtues of other peoples. It seems evident, then, that it is madness for anyone anywhere to console himself with the thought, "It can't happen here." It can—and others can attempt to excuse themselves with those same haunting sentences, "We were helpless. There was nothing we could do."

I think that there *was* something that could have been done in Germany. With more courage, more people, armed with the strength of conviction, could have resisted sooner and more effectively. It will be argued that earlier opposition would only have caused more blood to be spilled sooner. I do not think so. Spilled sooner, perhaps, but, for that reason, very possibly less blood. In any case, there would have been more honor and more truth, hence less degradation and less vileness. (Here I must say that I write not as a man of courage finding fault, but merely as a man who admires courage and appreciates its importance to the affairs of men.)

Though many fought fearlessly for freedom, there obviously was not enough courage in the hearts of enough people in Nazi Germany to stem the tide of evil. Why this was so I do not know. Perhaps no one does. Perhaps no one ever will. The point to be made, however, is simply that the courage to dare, to dare to stand up and be counted in times of crises—large or small, national, world-wide or local—is the only cure for much of the injustice and social suffering of the world. We need a lot more courage to dare.

Unfortunately for Americans, what has been happening in the South for the past few years is not entirely different from what happened in Germany twenty and twenty-five years ago. There are many decent Southerners who might also say, "We are helpless. There is nothing we can do." And within the framework of normal human life, and the lack of courage we all too often display, this is true.

Unfortunately for Northerners, what has been happening in the South in the past has now begun in the North as well. And the chances are that Northerners will run (as some have already) to hide behind the same tree where the people of the South have found shelter. I know, because I have hidden there myself. I live in New England where we have long pretended that there is no prejudice. When my ten year old son, who attends public school in a town where there is no segregation, came home and asked how come *all* the players on a rival school's baseball team were Negroes, I had to confess that I could not give him any satisfactory explanation. I tell myself that I am helpless. There is nothing I can do.

Even so, I know there is. It is not that people are confused about what is morally right. In most public issues involving morality enough people know what needs to be done to get it done. They just don't dare. (Some, of course, say they don't care. Either they are lying or they are beyond redemption.) The reasons for their fear vary; but almost always the fear is the thing that immobilizes them. Fear, being a child of the Devil, is a wily one and so masquerades in many forms and costumes. These he calls "explanations"; but stripped and shown in their true light, they turn out to be merely excuses.

We don't much like the Do-Gooder or the Espouser-of-Causes or the active joiner of citizens' committees. Such people bother our consciences. So we scorn them, criticize them, question their motives and their background and do everything else we can to cut them down to size—our size. But whatever else may be said about them, they do have the courage of their convictions and are willing to stand up for their convictions. Their courage upsets the rest of us, as it should. Out of fear, most of us like to insulate ourselves from unpleasantness, injustice, and the suffering of others, thinking thereby to be absolved from responsibility. All we are really doing is preparing ourselves for the day when we too can say, "We were helpless. There was nothing we could do."

I have spoken of two types of courage—or rather, two

situations that call for courage. But courage can be defined in many ways, and by looking at it from other angles one may deepen one's understanding of its nature.

The place to start is with physical courage, even though most of us think it is somewhat irrelevant to our own daily lives. Vaguely we realize that someday we may have to face a serious operation or feel the pain of a long illness. We know that accidents do happen and the day may come when we may be involved in, or witness, some accident which will suddenly call upon whatever physical courage we may possess. But most of the time we avoid thinking of such unpleasant possibilities and in practice live as though we really thought nothing painful would ever happen to us. So we relegate physical courage to the background as something belonging to the age of chivalry or the days of our Puritan ancestors. We muse about it at times; when we read of courage in the face of the tortures of the Inquisition, or the even more refined ones of the recent war years, we cannot help wondering how we would have behaved in such situations. Still, our musing is not soul-searching. We hope that we would have had sufficient courage, but we are not sure and we are not really worried. After all, we were never trained for this sort of thing. It is not an integral part of our education (football to the contrary not withstanding). Its elimination as a serious need for everyday life, we assume, is a sign of our advancing civilization. It was not so among the Greeks, however, nor among the American Indians, nor among the cavaliers of medieval times. With them it *was* a part of the training for life. And they may have been right.

Courage

Whether they were or not, it is necessary for us to remember that physical courage is the classic form, most universally understood and most universally appreciated. Even in our day, and always in the past, it is a bond of decency among men—and in some situations the only bond—for men almost always admire physical courage in another, even an enemy.

As part of his heritage, the Christian should certainly remember the overwhelmingly important role which physical courage played in the early history of his faith. It started with the Crucifixion itself, continued through the ages, and has written some glorious chapters in more than one corner of the earth in our day. Much of the early and astonishingly rapid growth of the Christian Church was directly attributable to the great physical courage of its adherents as they endured stones and imprisonment and torture and death. Casual and uncommitted observers were at first moved to curiosity, then to admiration, and at last to commitment.

Finally, we need to remember that physical courage forces upon a man an evaluation of life itself. By definition it always implies a threat to his body, and by logical extension, therefore, ultimately a choice between life and death at some price or other. Thus he will find the physical courage to risk injury, pain and perhaps even death directly in accordance with his philosophy of life. If that philosophy eschews thought in favor of action, then he will find the physical courage to drive racing cars and parachute out of airplanes for fun. If that philosophy is more concerned with moral commitments, if a person is a man of conscience, then he may be the one to say, "There are some things I cannot accept. I would rather die than endorse them." For such a man

Courage

the time may come when he will have to decide what those things are, and the physical courage he then musters will be the measure of his conviction. Until the nature of physical courage has been seriously examined, no other kind of courage can be understood or appreciated. Not only is it the prototype; it is the parent, the origin of the species.

More familiar to us, however, and closer at hand is moral courage. Insofar as physical courage plays a part in our lives at all, it is usually in the form of the courage to bear. Moral courage, in our life and times, more often takes the form of courage to dare. Whether we have passed or failed, we have all been tested on this score many times, and on many different levels of importance. Those of us whose physical courage has not yet been tested can only wonder what strength we might show. But about our moral courage we have a rather clear (though not necessarily accurate) picture. For a better understanding, however, it is best to look beyond ourselves.

Fortunately, courage in this form, as in the first, is something which we tend to admire in others, even in those with whom we disagree. During the last war, conscientious objectors, small minority that they were, commanded the admiration of many for their moral courage. And, to take an example from an entirely difference area, John F. Kennedy, in his book *Profiles In Courage* was able to write a fine chapter on Robert Taft, a political opponent. (By a strange coincidence, that sentence was written one day before Mr. Kennedy's assassination. His death caused millions of friends and enemies alike—some for the first time—to realize that when this man wrote of courage he wrote as an authority.) Wherever we discover true moral courage—in friend, stranger, or enemy, we find it admirable. And so we should, for along with love it is the most powerful and effective force for good in human history. Again and again it has stemmed the tide or turned the corner from waywardness to a better way.

It is fashionable, and it is easy to find fault with our age. It is usual to point (with pride in one's own cleverness) to the countless examples of our immorality or our amorality. But such an enumeration is only half the story. Heroes still walk the earth—men who are strong morally, moral martyrs and some moral victors. In the struggle for civil rights which today is wracking our country, the villains command most of the newsprint and are most photographed. But there are as many heroes—I think many more—and they are certain to win the day in the long run. When they do, we can at least hope that the historians will right the wrongs of the journalists. But if they don't, it will not matter much. Moral courage will have won the day—and if it is a victory of anonymous heroes, it will not be the first time. Nobody is really fooled. Everyone knows that there is such a thing as moral courage, that it has always been and will always be a power for good. That cynicism and pessimism often have a better press is just in the nature of things. Sometimes the world is blessed with moral giants, leaders like Jeremiah and Amos and Lincoln and Churchill. But mostly moral courage is quiet. Let no man be lulled thereby into thinking that it has vanished or that it has become outmoded. One could do worse than to call to mind one from his own list of morally brave men each day before picking up the morning paper and reading of the Devil and all his works.

A third type of courage is perhaps more a part of our

Courage

daily lives than any of the others. Let us call it social courage. It is really a part of moral courage, but, since it appears to be on such an entirely different level of importance, it should perhaps be treated separately. Generally we take it less seriously than it deserves.

Social courage is the courage to dare to say what we really believe when we do not have to, and when to do so may make us unpopular for the moment. I am sure that for the sake of sociability we often say things we do not believe. More often, by our agreement or even by our silence we condone things others say which we do not believe—as though sociability were itself a virtue instead of (as is often the case) merely a product of our fear that we shall be ill-thought-of by others, including too often those whose opinions we neither share nor admire. The guilt here is widespread. I confess. As a matter of principle, for example, I happen to have a strong aversion to all jokes playing upon the so-called characteristics of the Jews. I think it is wrong to tell them, wrong to laugh at them, and even wrong to listen to them. And yet I too often have not had the social courage to voice my objections—except from the safety of the pulpit or the printed page. I also have an aversion to sweeping condemnations of either of our two great political parties, such as extremists on both sides invariably make in the heat of battle and sometimes gratuitously between elections. I believe such people are almost invariably uninformed, unintelligent, un-American, destructive, and self-centered. They are also usually vicious. Yet, again, I have listened silently many hours on end in my life to such offensive talk by pathetic people trying so desperately to attract attention. In tolerating these and other offenses I think I am no better and no worse than countless others (otherwise

I would not have been so willing to confess). The socially courageous are not numerous, from which fact we might deduce, "Maybe it's not so important." Rather, we should deduce, "Maybe it is not so easy."

Nobody really admires a gossip. Everyone agrees that idle chatter about other people is an unattractive trait, that it is never entirely harmless, and that it can sometimes be cruel and extremely devastating. So let us consign the inveterate gossip to hell. That is easy to do because the inveterate gossip is always on the *other* side of the back fence. Having done that, however, let us admit that the occasional gossip—a title which very few of us can escape—deserves censure too, more severe censure, perhaps, than many people may think is called for. In a small way, gossip is like murder. Anyone who goes around murdering people every day is a wicked person. But the fact that such people exist does not lessen the guilt of those who kill just a *few* people, now and then. The point is that it is wrong to kill. And of course everybody knows it.

This brings us to the question of *condonation*. Gossip is the easiest sin in the world to eradicate. All one has to do is refuse to take part in it—either to join in or to listen. There can be no gossip unless there is someone standing on *each* side of the back fence. It takes two or more people for gossip to prosper. But to combat gossip takes courage—social courage—more of it than most of us seem to possess. And, if social courage is the least glamorous form of courage, and of itself perhaps the least important, surely the opportunities to practice it are most numerous. Hardly a day passes without affording each of us the chance to test himself. Social courage begins with the *condemnation* of gossip.

Social courage is a tricky thing, for there are so many

Courage

ways that a man can fool himself about it. He can tell himself that, in such and such company, it is just useless to argue or that the issue of the moment is just not all that important (social harmony being considered more so) or that common courtesy demands that he keep still or say he agrees. As a rule, we underestimate the importance of social courage. When social courage fails, it leaves a most insidious opening for cowardliness. Like all other sins, cowardliness begins innocently—among a few friends and in matters of little importance. Then it spreads unnoticed to larger moral issues. We so easily delude ourselves, thinking that the greater the issue the more courage we shall be able to muster. When we really need it, we think, we shall have it. We think so, but we won't. Jesus said, "The man who can be trusted in little things can be trusted also in great; and the man who is dishonest in little things is dishonest also in great things." He was speaking then of worldly goods, but what He said is true also of courage.

The source of human courage is not hidden. It is implied in much that has been said in this discussion and is most clearly revealed in that most common of phrases, the courage of conviction. Courage comes from faith. It is one of the fairest deals God ever made with man. We are in the habit of saying, "It takes courage" to live by one's convictions. But the deal is better than that. Through one's convictions courage is *given*, and the relationship between the two is direct. The amount of courage is merely a thermometer, measuring the exact heat of the conviction, for a man's courage is tempered in that heat. If, as we often say, courage is cool, it is cool like steel. There has been heat. In my own life I

Courage

think of two opportunities presented to me to be courageous—both, as it happened, demanding physical courage. When I was a sophomore in college, I got a job as a bouncer at the twenty-fifth reunion for the Class of 1911. I was supposed to keep out gate-crashing undergraduates. The first to try to slip in were two seniors, both of whom I recognized immediately. One was captain of the wrestling team and the other was captain of the boxing team. They were two of the nicest fellows I knew and both illustrated my father's old saying, "A gentleman is a gentleman, drunk or sober." I just had no stomach for my job and didn't see why they should not join such a lovely party. So I found something to occupy me somewhere else until the head man could take over. About twenty years later I redeemed myself. Wooster School was having its senior prom and a gang from a local high school came out, lead by the captain of the football team, a monstrous and notoriously mean young man who could have killed me. But with my jaw out a mile, I marched up to him, took him *firmly* by the arm and led him straight off the campus, to the astonishment of the boys of Wooster, who never knew until that moment that I was really quite a hero. That time I had the courage of my conviction, and my poor opponent had no particular convictions that night and so was quite meek and mild.

To say, of course, that the source of courage is conviction is to say that everybody in the world has courage at some time or other, under some circumstance or other, since there is no one who is without *any* convictions. Jesus said, "Where your wealth is, there will your heart be also." And the French word for heart is "coeur," from which comes the English word "courage." Everyone is courageous about the things that matter most to him, about the things that he believes in most passionately, that are most precious to him. If it is one's own life, a person will fight courageously for that. If it is the life of a child, he will fight with the courage of a she-bear for that, even at the risk of losing his own. If it is a "treasure in heaven," then the promise is that the courage for that will also be provided, that no thief may be able to approach, no moth corrupt.

What determines a man's courage is the frequency and type of issue about which he is courageous. Since, under one circumstance or another every man may have courage, what we mean by a courageous man is one whose courage is exercised more often on a more inclusive range of issues than most. Here, almost by definition, the religious man excels. If it could be said of a certain man that he has deep-seated convictions about the sacredness of life—his own and others, about human suffering, about morality, about meaning and purpose in human history and about neighborliness, it would almost have to be said of that man that he is religious. At least such an all-embracing set of convictions is most commonly found within the framework of fairly orthodox religious belief—the more inclusive the convictions the more likely they are to be based on religious belief. It would also have to follow that such a man would normally be expected to be more courageous, more often, about a greater variety of issues than a man with a shallower and less inclusive set of convictions. He would have to be a courageous man. If there is a God, courage comes from God. Whenever any man is courageous it is because—whether he acknowledges it or not at the time—he is in touch with

God. And whoever most closely and most often and most reverently puts himself in touch with God—as best he may—will most often and most decisively be given courage. It's free—to those who believe.

Each of these facts about man... their differences—will never often and most clearly give themselves freely to those who belong.

Isolation

To men the sheep in a herd look so much alike that it is hard to tell one from another, but to a sheep men look so much alike that no doubt it is equally hard for him to tell one man from another. However we may be offended by the thought, it is true that we do have a very great many things in common; we are *very* much alike, so much so that even though we presumably have more discernment than sheep, we sometimes have trouble ourselves telling each other apart. If one were to list all of the qualities and characteristics that belong solely to man, it would be a long and significant list.

At the same time, we know very well that no two men in the entire history of the world—which includes some billions of individuals—have ever been exactly alike. Every man is a unique creature.

Each of these facts about man has implications of vast importance, but it is the last, man's uniqueness, which most concerns me here. Because he is unique, every man is separate—and therefore isolated—from every other man on earth. He has ties with others—of blood, of interest, and of affection. But a tie by its very nature and function, is a symbol not of oneness but of separation. A boat is tied to a dock, but boat and dock remain two different things. A husband and wife are tied together by marriage vows, but they remain different individuals. Friends are sometimes so close that they are said to be inseparable, but they are never indistinguishable. Blood brothers, of course, are notorious for their differences. The late Horace Taft had a story about an unlettered farm boy who made this point wonderfully clear. "Me and my brother ain't any more alike than if we wasn't us, and he's just as different as me, only the other way." Each man, by his uniqueness, is separated from all the rest of the world. He is isolated, set apart, distinct.

Paradoxically, since this separateness is true of *all* men, it is one of the things they have in common, a natural and universal characteristic which should be no more troublesome than the simple fact of being alive. But there is a uniqueness to each man's uniqueness. We are all "just as different" as everybody else, but each in his own way. So, by the quality and the degree and the cause of our isolation, we are each presented with problems with which we must cope, sometimes as a permanent condition of our existence and sometimes as a temporary one. Because no two human situations are exactly alike, it is hard to generalize even about the isolation we all have in common. However, by using three different words to illustrate three different kinds and qualities of isolation, we may be able to clarify the total concept. These three words are *loneliness, aloneness*, and *solitude*. Admittedly these divisions are arbitrary, over-simplified, and therefore somewhat decep-

tive. Every kind of isolation is colored to some extent
with every other kind.

Nevertheless let us start with loneliness. This is a sad
word. It sounds sad when it is spoken and it always
seems to come from deep in one's throat, usually with
the trace of a catch. It elicits pity, for someone else or
for one's self. Whatever the cause, loneliness *is* sad, the
saddest form of human isolation. It means always to
have an aching heart, to be continually on the point of
tears. It means not to be understood and not to understand. It means not to belong, to suffer a need unful-
filled. It is not good to be lonely.

There are many causes of loneliness, but perhaps the
most poignant is the loneliness of simple circumstance.
Those who live in families, however they may sometimes fight and whatever their problems of living together may be, too seldom take time to think with
sympathy and understanding of those who are forced
to live a solitary life. Never having lived alone, I speak
with no authority, but it is not very difficult to imagine
the aching loneliness of hundreds of thousands of people on this earth, who live by themselves and go home
from work each day to an empty house or room and a
meal prepared and eaten in silence. And how much
worse is the plight of those who are too old or too
feeble to work, who do not even have the respite of a
few hours of useful business in the world while the sun
is up, five days a week.

Temporary isolation is not as fearsome as endless
loneliness, but it is not necessarily less painful while
it lasts. Though its terminus may in fact be discernible
in the distance, emotion so often dims his eye that the

victim cannot see. So is it with the first experience of homesickness. A boy or girl away at boarding school or college for the first time, or a young man off in the service, may know the exact date of his first vacation or leave. But even having a calendar with the days marked off clearly doesn't help. What good does it do to count the days when each day is an eternity? The emotional tangle can be so great that reason has no chance to fight its way through. "I'm lonesome!" is the pathetic cry, and nothing in the world makes sense. A whole family can sometimes feel the pangs together. Those who have moved into a community where they know not a soul are familiar with the feeling. And if they should be in a strange land, speaking a foreign tongue, their loneliness is all the worse. Such people, far from home, suddenly become aware of the hundreds of supports that friends and associates and familiar people at home had provided to help them to stand upright. Now they feel alone, and lonely. This loneliness will not last, of course, but who can believe that while the pain is so great?

Deserving the most compassion are the numerous souls separated from the rest of the world by some physical affliction. One's heart goes out to those so ill or crippled that they can never leave their houses, the people who in some churches are gracelessly called "shut-ins." But perhaps they are actually less desolate than those whose afflictions are not bad enough to keep them from going out, only bad enough to keep them from being *asked*. Sympathy so often has such delicate sensibilities; it likes to respond to *attractive* sadness. A famous story begins thus:

Isolation

There was once a rich man, who dressed in purple and the finest linen, and feasted in great magnificence every day. At his gate, covered with sores, lay a poor man named Lazarus, who would have been glad to satisfy his hunger with the scraps from the rich man's table. Even the dogs used to come and lick his sores.

I think it was not the poverty of Lazarus which hardened the rich man's heart so much as his sores. Many of our fellow humans are isolated by physical deformities which so offend our sensibilities that sympathy slinks away and we consign them to loneliness.

Through sheer circumstance, through no fault of their own whatever, countless people just do not belong. They are lonely.

But suppose it is not just circumstance. Suppose the fault is theirs. Does it matter very much? Is the loneliness therefore less? On the contrary, now it is even worse; for now the rest of the world feels free not merely to ignore and neglect but to blame. Consider sin. Here the separation is compounded and complete. It has often been said that sin is separation from God. It is also separation from one's fellow man and from one's proper self. If the sin is known, there is ostracism, one of the cruelest acts of man to man. The punishment, of course, depends upon the sinfulness of the sin in the eyes of the rest of the community. Each community has its own list of pardonable and unpardonable sins. In the world of a boys' school, for example, the unpardonable sins are stealing, cheating, squealing, and letting someone else take the rap. For these a guilty boy can be pretty thoroughly ostracized and left severely alone. In the various adult worlds the lists are different; but, if one world is puzzled by the inclusions and omissions of another, the feeling is always reciprocated. In any case, when the sin is known, and when it is deemed unpardonable, the sinner is left heartlessly lonely.

When the sin is secret, however, the loneliness goes even deeper, since it is in secret that loneliness hurts most. Now sin's separation becomes overwhelming indeed. To walk into a room full of people one knows and to be wholly ignored, to be made pointedly to feel that one does not belong, is to feel some pangs of loneliness. But to walk into that same room and be greeted with open arms, *as though one really did belong,* knowing in his heart that he does not, is to plumb the depths of the misery of human isolation. The first compares with the second as the part of the iceberg above the water compares with that below the surface.

When we consider the apparently unpaid-for sins of others, we tend to bitterness. "He gets away with murder. . . ." we say. "Why should he always get off scot-free?" But when we consider our own sins, for which—by the same measure—we have never paid, we know this is not true. Sin is its own worst punishment, and the more hidden the sin, the more devastating the inward penalty. Perhaps there are some with hearts so hard they do not feel the pain, but I do not believe it. How did their hearts get so hard? Was it not from just such pain?

I, for one, hope that there is a purgatory in the hereafter, where I may have a chance to work off at least some of my sins before my case is heard. And I think there must be, for I am sure there is Justice in God's Mercy, as well as Mercy in His Justice. It seems clear from our experiences here on earth not only that we need both but that we need each touched with the other. Meanwhile, until we seek help in the only place where it can be found, for our secret sins we pay the price of the worst kind of loneliness known to man.

Last on the list of this kind of isolation is self-pity. Here indeed the Devil is at work. Everything about self-pity is bad, and like all other evil it is fascinatingly tempting. Loneliness puts its roots down deep in the soil of self-pity. It blossoms like a thistle in the sunshine of self-pity, and grows and multiplies and grows again. Self-pity forms such a high, gateless wall around the lush patch of loneliness that no gardener may ever enter to pull the awful weeds.

How ironic, too, since the gardener who would most like to enter and set things right is pity. Pity and self-pity are related. Like Isaac and Ishmael, the sons of Abraham, they are half-brothers. The circumstances of their births set Isaac and Ishmael against one another. Abraham's wife, Sarah, was barren, and in her shame suggested that her husband father a child by her maid, Hagar. It was a noble gesture on Sarah's part, but a poor arrangement that did little credit to Abraham. But he felt sorry for himself, so Ishmael was born to Hager, the child of Abraham's self-pity. Then God had pity on Abraham and so Isaac was born to Sarah herself. Isaac, the child of God's pity, and Ishmael, the child of Abraham's self-pity, became sworn enemies for life. And so are they still. In resentment and sinful pride we cry out to our best friends when we are in distress, "I don't want your pity!", having not quite honesty or perception enough to add, "I prefer my own." So loneliness is nourished by self-pity, which, in turn, is fed by loneliness.

Whether forced upon one by circumstances or rooted

in his own blind wilfulness, loneliness is always sad. For some it is a permanent condition of life and at some time or other it is at least a chapter in the life of every man. But always it is sad. That it is bearable, that it can be borne with courage and grace, that it can even be dispelled—more often than we sometimes realize—these are the assurances and affirmations of faith.

Here it is not only the *presence* of faith, it is the *quality* of faith that is all-important. It must be personal; it must be revealed; it must have mystery; it must have presence. It begins and ends with prayer, which is at the same time faith's ultimate expression and its source of renewal. Prayer is so fundamental and vast a subject that to treat it at all properly would require a book in itself—and fortunately many excellent ones have been written on prayer. Here and now I want only to try and clarify the relevance of prayer to the efficacy of faith, particularly as regards loneliness.

The story of Elijah and the prophets of Baal seems a good place to begin. It is in many ways a primitive story but, like many others in the Old Testament, it is full of insights and revealed truth. King Ahab had been persuaded by his wife, Jezebel, to forsake the God of his fathers and to worship Baal instead. As is usually the case, abandoning God didn't seem to make much difference at first. But eventually there came a severe drought. Something had to be done. It was time to decide who really was God; so a praying contest was planned between the prophets of Baal, four hundred and fifty strong, and Elijah—alone. Each prepared sacrifices to be burned. But no fires were lit. Each side was to pray to its God to produce fire by a miracle. And the miracle would be followed, of course, by rain.

The prophets of Baal were first and after their sacrifice was prepared they began to pray. "O Baal, answer us! But there was no voice, and no one answered." Elijah began to ridicule them. "Cry aloud, for he is a god; either he is musing, or he has gone aside, or he is on a journey, or perhaps he is asleep and must be awakended." The prophets of Baal tried again, but without success. "There was no voice; no one answered, no one heeded."

Elijah had better luck. Immediately after he started to pray, the fire descended and lit the sacrifice and the people all cried, "The Lord, he is God; the Lord, he is God." And after that came the rain. But that was not the end of the story. Jezebel heard about the contest— and the fact that all the prophets of Baal had summarily been put to death—and she was determined to destroy Elijah. Like all prophets, even successful ones (perhaps especially successful ones), Elijah's day in the sun was short. He had been an outcast before, and now he became a fugitive. He fled to the wilderness, by himself, and began to pray in earnest this time—not for show, but for his own soul.

Alone and afraid, Elijah was not so sure of himself as he had been. Nor were his prayers so readily answered this time. Forty days and forty nights he wandered alone in the wilderness, until he came to Horeb, the mount of God. There he hid in a cave, while outside God showed His might. There was wind and earthquake and fire. "But the Lord was not in the wind . . . not in the earthquake . . . not in the fire." But after the fire, "a still small voice." This Elijah heard and "wrapped his face in his mantle and went out and stood in the entering in of the cave" and prepared himself to go back into the world and continue with his appointed tasks there.

Isolation

For the purpose of this discussion, it might be well to set aside the burned offerings and the rain and the wind and the earthquake and the fire. What is left is the very essence of religious faith. It starts with the cry of the people. "The Lord, he is God; the Lord, he is God." But long before the people uttered that cry, Elijah had believed in God. That is the real point of the story, and of all religious faith.

Most of us are not Elijahs, nor are we prophets of Baal. We are the people, "limping with two different opinions," as Elijah put it. So we must expect, when we pray, that there will be many times when there will be no voice, no one answering, no one heeding. Even Elijah, when he got around to his own private praying, prayed day after day and night after night and must have been scared half out of his wits by God's pyrotechnics before he finally heard the "still small voice." Jesus Himself, on the Mount of Olives, prayed not without difficulty, saying, " 'Father, if it be thy will, take this cup away from me. Yet not my will but thine be done.' . . . and in anguish of spirit he prayed the more urgently; and his sweat was like clots of blood falling to the ground." One might well paraphrase for prayer what was once said of Christianity itself, "It is not that prayer has been tried and found wanting, rather that it has been found difficult and not tried."

What the theologians call the practice of the presence of God is a daily discipline for the faithful. It is easy for no one, and there are seldom quick rewards. But, as it is the essence of faith, so is it the crown. For the lonely it is the strength to bear. More than that, it is the antidote. For to be alone with God is to be alone without being lonely. Thomas à Kempis has written, "Christ shall come and give you His consoling presence,

179

if from within you have prepared a place where He may fitly dwell." For those with faith enough to believe that such can be, for those willing to pray without ceasing that it shall be, there is no loneliness.

But isolation takes other forms, not so sad. One I would label *to be alone*. Perhaps I bend language too arbitrarily to my purpose, but by this phrase I mean to suggest a different category of isolation from loneliness, a state which is sober but not sad. Two common human situations may serve as examples: sorrow and decision.

Sorrow itself, of course, is sad. But the aloneness of sorrow is not sad. When first a man is in sorrow, his natural reaction is to reach out for help, and the natural reaction of friends is to offer it. Such gestures do help. In times of stress it is good and comforting to know that others care. But is it not strange that there is more yearning in the hearts of those who stand by to help than in the heart of the afflicted one? Friends positively plead to "do something." And the kinds of things they do symbolize the truth of the situation all too eloquently. They send flowers and write letters and bring in covered dishes of things to eat; they volunteer to answer the telephone and sometimes they even "make arrangements." Occasionally the onslaught of determined helpfulness would be funny if it were not sad. Neighbors almost literally knock each other over in order to get there first to carry out some simple assignment, the primary usefulness of which is simply to make *them* feel as though they were being useful. A wise mourner lets them. Two or three neighbors come to call. While they are in the living room, the doorbell rings. They all leap to their feet. In a trice the winner is obvious, so the others turn to the bereaved to be first with the next best thing—meaningless words. "Now don't you worry about a thing. You just sit still and relax. We'll take care of everything for you." The winner returns. "It was a wire from Sally. I signed for it." (Hands it over and waits.) "Lovely, isn't it? I'll make a note of it. . . . Don't thank me! After all, what are friends and neighbors for?"

Friends and neighbors are just for that and no more, and it is good. They can help to do everything—except bear the pain. That, a man or woman must do alone. Even a husband cannot help a wife, or a son a father, or a mother a daughter. Sorrow is so personal that it completely separates the sorrowing from all the rest of the world. Each mourner stands utterly alone. If he has never stood there before, he may be afraid. But soon he learns that, however sad the situation, the aloneness itself is not sad.

Using the word "lonely" not as I have defined it here but in the sense that I use "alone," Bernard Shaw, in *St. Joan,* expresses the truth, through Joan's own lips. "I see now that the loneliness of God is His strength." It is man's strength too. It would be indecent if it were otherwise, for behind sorrow are a man's most intimate and secret feelings and his most personal relationships. Not only *must* he bear his sorrow by himself, but he finds he *wants* to. And in that wanting is the beginning of his strength. Perhaps he would like to bare his soul to his very closest friend or lover, but in his heart of hearts (where his soul stands guard against just such intrusions) he knows that he cannot. Almost by definition a man's soul is just that part of him which cannot be laid bare. So he must stand alone, and so standing, little by little feels his strength, *his own* strength, holding him upright. This is sober, but not sad.

The advantage to the believer is that he can have it

two ways. Only a man of faith can be alone and yet
not alone. To God he does not have to bother to try to
bare his soul, for God is that Being, alone, "unto whom
all hearts are open, all desires known and from whom
no secrets are hid." Such a One, and only such a One,
can provide help exactly as help is needed.

Decision is not so different from sorrow, though it
has a greater variety of forms. A man in middle life,
with a successful career and a happy home and everything organized just the way he used to hope it might
be someday, is asked to consider changing everything
in order to take on what is presented to him as "a challenge." There are so many things to take into account:
the happiness of his wife and children, and his own,
and whether or not this new thing is indeed a challenge.
He seeks advice from everyone who will listen, close
friends and mere acquaintances and perhaps a perfect
stranger standing next to him at a bar. With them he
examines the issues over and over again, arriving each
time at a different answer. More secretly he also examines his own motives, and, if he is really honest, in the
end he admits to himself that they are all mixed and
all a little suspect. Little by little it becomes clear to
him that eventually he is going to have to stop talking
to people and go off by himself and make up his own
mind. For a while he puts off that fearful day with all
kinds of ratiocinations about how particularly valuable
this or that person's advice would be. But when he
finally does get off by himself—utterly alone—he learns
that being alone is not so frightening as he had expected. Once again he begins to feel his own strength.

Another man in authority is faced with what is to
me one of the most terrifying decisions in this world,

firing someone else from his job. Again the haunting questions: Is it really necessary? Is the smooth running of the organization really that important? What will it do to the man and to his family? Is the record straight? And, worst of all, can I bring myself to look him in the eye and tell him? (And I think that any man in authority who ever fires a man or woman except face-to-face is an inexcusable coward.) Again there is the urge to seek the advice and counsel and comfort of others. And again the truth becomes clearer and clearer: this is a decision which at last must be made alone. However agonizing the decision, it is right to make it alone and only alone. In this aloneness there is strength. It is the quintessence of what people call responsibility.

A woman is married to a man who drinks too much, or carouses too much, or works too little. Furthermore, he adds insult to injury as well as injury to insult by punishing his wife and perhaps his children whenever he is in the house. The situation disintegrates, never suddenly but always tantalizingly little by little. Should she leave him? Would separation really be better for the children? Would it be her own salvation? Might it not even be his salvation? From close friends she too seeks advice. And she too finds that advice is not decision. It is free, and too often worth just that price. She too must decide alone. And only when she is prepared to stand alone will she find the strength.

There are many in the world who admire what they call "a man of decision," a man who can instantly see all sides of a situation, evaluate them and with his decisive mind reach a quick conclusion. There are others, admirers of Hamlet, who suspect that the decision-maker is either too stupid to see how complicated the issues really are or too insensitive to care. The truth lies between. This world requires that decisions be made, many of them of vast importance and very few of them between pure black and pure white. If he is worthy of the decision he is to make, the decision-maker agonizes alone—always alone. It is a very sober process, but it cannot and it ought not to be otherwise.

Prayer has for many centuries and in many religions and cultures been an accepted part of the process of making decisions. Of course it has often been cheapened, desecrated, used for show. But nothing can be desecrated unless it is in essence sacred, and surely the long association between prayer and decision bears witness to some sacredness. It takes a hardened cynic to believe that prayer in such a context is always for window dressing, only as a pledge of sincerity or witness to rightness. When a man, in the agony of decision, cries out, "O God, help me!", God just might take him at his word and help him. He won't make his decision for him, but as The Authority On Aloneness, He might show him where strength may be found. And the better He is known the more help He will be able to give. God never says absolutely "No," even to the novice's prayer of desperation. The college boy who writes his father only when he needs money will usually get it. The father is almost compelled to send it, just because he is a father. But a richer correspondence would make for a deeper relationship and a wider variety of kinds of helpfulness. So the religious man—the man whose faith is a daily reality—is better served in sorrow or decision than the man whose faith is less.

If loneliness is sad and aloneness sober, then solitude, the third form of human isolation, is glorious. Primarily it is glorious in its creativity. Most people think that art is one of the hallmarks of humanity. And the artist almost always—no, always—creates only when he separates himself altogether from his fellow man. Usually, in fact, this separation must be symbolized by actual physical solitude, though some rare men seem to be able to achieve solitude even when surrounded by other people. So the painter or sculptor repairs to his studio and the author shuts himself up in his den (or "in the tunnel," as a writer friend of mine puts it), and the musician goes off alone with his instrument. Even the preacher, though he performs in public, prepares and practices by himself.

Man, by nature, we say, is a gregarious animal, craving togetherness above all else. But that is only a half truth. Everybody laughed when Greta Garbo said, "I want to be alone," but much of the crassness of Hollywood springs from its utter inability to understand what she meant. For man is not wholly a gregarious animal. Perhaps, he is gregarious only insofar as he is an animal. But that part of him which craves solitude is a precious and glorious part of him, and very particularly a part of his non-animal humanity. It is in solitude that his soul soars until man is just a little "lower than the angels." In solitude he learns to command colors and notes and words. To be sure, his works serve to bring his fellows together—with him and with each other. But, the more deeply and thoroughly people understand the processes of the artist's creativity, the more profoundly will they glory in their own solitude.

One doesn't have to be a talented artist to feel the power of solitude. Most men do their best thinking when lying awake in the darkest hours of night, when everyone else is asleep—and it matters very little whether that best be something special or not. Thinking itself, whether done in the middle of a public meeting or in a class or alone at night or early in the morning, is perhaps the most solitary activity of man— and one of the most magnificent. While he thinks, a man is isolated completely from the rest of the world. Of a silent one we often say, "He is lost in thought." He is not lost. It is we who are lost. He may just at that very moment have *found* something of himself. The isolation of solitude is precious and there are few who do not crave it, now and then, and a little more *now* than their sometimes frantic-seeming joinings together would indicate.

Some say there is no art which is not religious; and with them I confess I stand. A lecturer once flashed on a projection screen a picture of a derelict—poor, neglected, hungry, dirty, and degenerate. The background was a fabulous city, rich in its beauty and in its gaudiness alike. The lecturer asked the class, "Is that a religious picture?" After much heated discussion, it was agreed that it was. One way to make certain that anyone could agree with the opening sentence of this paragraph is to define the word "religious" so broadly that it is all-inclusive. Then there can be no argument. And in a sense this is not so far from the mark. Surely there are some religious overtones in Van Gogh's portrait of the postman, and even more in some portraits of himself. Anything that has to do with life has some religious relevance. So does anything that has to do with death. Throw in beauty and ugliness, joy and sorrow, and the fields of art are pretty well covered.

But I would like to be more specific. I would like to

say that the more precisely and directly and overtly a work of art is religious the more *opportunity* it has for greatness. I submit for evidence the Cathedral of Chartres and I contend—very subjectively, I admit—not only that part of its greatness is its religiousness but that part of its *artistic* greatness is its religiousness. I would say the same of the best of Italian Renaissance painting and the poetry of the Psalms and the Gospel of John and *Paradise Lost* and the music of Bach.

For me the reason is not far to seek. To create, a man separates himself from his fellow man and works in solitude. In that solitude, and in the act of creating, he is setting the stage for the closest possible relationship with the Author of all of Creation. To the extent that he believes that, his solitude and its creativity may be filled with beauty and glory. Knowing how hard and conscientiously much of the art world of today has tried to separate itself from this very thesis, I am sure my statement will be criticized. I am comforted, however, by the thought that, in my own eyes at least, I am "compassed about with so great a cloud of witnesses."

The isolation of any human from the rest of the world for any length of time and for any cause presents a problem, a problem of vast importance. It must be borne with grace, it must be understood with strength, or it must be used creatively. The late Dr. Allen O. Whipple, for years one of the world's leading surgeons, was the greatest man it has ever been my privilege to know personally. As a professor of surgery and a high-ranking hospital executive, as a writer and painter and on several occasions as a man of sorrow, he experienced many kinds of human isolation. Though a man belonging to the world and in constant service to his fellow man, he well knew what it meant to be lonely and to be alone and to be in solitude. I never knew anyone who coped so successfully with all these types of situations, who bore them with such grace and understanding and glory. Dr. Whipple was a deeply religious man. I believe that all these facts, most pointedly the last, are relevant to each other. I will go further. I believe that most such men are men of faith. And I think when you find a person who is truly great, you will say: There is a deeply religious man.

Self

"He is his own worst enemy," is a common way of describing a friend. Whether charitably or uncharitably said, it is almost always the truth. Nearly everyone is his own worst enemy, for of all the human problems I have discussed, none compares in difficulty and persistency with the problem of handling one's self. " 'To thine own self be true,' " wrote a modern commentator, "is a first-class bit of drivel which Shakespeare quite rightly put into the mouth of one of his greatest fools." As advice, especially to the young, it is surely drivel. Nevertheless it has an extraordinarily subtle appeal which has made it one of Shakespeare's most quoted lines. By presenting as the ideal simple reality as it exists, Shakespeare has lured the unwary into uncritical agreement. No advice seems sounder to most people than that which they themselves think they do not need. Most people *are* true to themselves, all too true, all too preoccupied, all too concerned. So they are all too quick to accept the notion that intuitively they have been right all along and that their very self is and ought to be the touchstone of morality.

Jesus said, "Thou shalt love thy neighbor as thyself," the implications and presuppositions of which are exactly the opposite of Polonius' advice to Laertes. Starting with the assumption that most of the world is already all-too-true to itself, Jesus merely used the love of self (without at that moment indicating whether such self-affection was right or wrong) as the best possible illustration of what one's attitude and feelings ought to be toward others. Clearly, we love our self in such a complete and uncritical way that it is wholly sufficient to illustrate what our love for our neighbor ought to be. But the words "thou shalt" constitute a command, suggesting that it by no means "follows as the night the day" that we cannot then be false to any man. If it did, there would be no need for a command. That there is such a need—that it is indeed a desperate need—is emphasized by the fact that this is not just *a* command, but rather one of the two most important commands upon which the entire Christian ethic depends. What Jesus is saying is that we *ought* to love our neighbor the way we *do* love ourselves. At the root of the problem—and this is what makes most of us "our own worst enemy,"—is the fact that we cannot seem to make the transfer that is demanded by this commandment. We cannot love our neighbor the way we love ourselves, nor can we stop the inordinance with which we love ourselves.

Important as is the proper love of our neighbor, the concern here is with the improper love of self. I say that both in difficulty and significance this is a problem of the first magnitude for almost everyone in the world.

Self

It is my conviction, however, that like so many others, it is a problem peculiarly susceptible to the ministrations of religious faith.

What is a self? To begin with, the very word is a short, ugly, deformed, little thing. It is like a child which only a mother could love. The average self is so pinched, so wrinkled, so twisted, so dried up, so proud, so conceited, so craven, so obnoxious, that no one could possibly love it except itself. The self is the worst thing about most people, though this fact is a secret which quite a few people have learned to conceal very well from the rest of the world.

How does the average man love his self? He looks at his natural face in the glass and straightway forgets what manner of man he is. Isn't it odd that when one looks at someone *else* in the mirror *his* nose is always crooked, but one's own is not? I know there is some logical explanation for this illusion, but that all of us are fooled is a startling and suggestive fact just the same. Most of us cannot even be honest with ourselves about the way we look. Except for that first horrible glance early in the morning, we are generally rather pleased with what we see when we look in the mirror. This is how we love our self.

If we are so kind about our physical appearance (which, after all, the world can see and judge for itself) think how tender we are with the more secret aspects of our self. Almost invariably we give our self credit for every good motive, and when things go wrong, we provide every available excuse for our self. We have such long memories for our every good deed and such short memories for our sins and failures. There is a strange reflection of this in the way some Protestants

criticize the Roman Catholic practice of private confession on the grounds that the sins are too quickly and
easily forgiven—that is, they seem to think, wiped out
and eliminated as though they never had been committed. But even for the most irregular of Roman Cath-
olics, there is at least a reminder from time to time and
for the more faithful once a week. For most Protestants,
however, by some much more mysterious and inde-
fensible process, the slate is wiped cleaner sooner. (We
just forget it.) There are, of course, times when we pass
judgment on our self with some sternness. But such
judgment is usually tempered with infinite mercy. This
is how we love our self.

How tenaciously we protect every aspect of our self.
Our opinions, however hastily formed, are sacred to
us. We defend them against all comers, sacrificing courtesy and kindness toward friend and stranger, sometimes even love of wife and family. We disapprove of
ridicule when it is turned against others, of course, but
we positively hate it when it is applied to ourselves.
Generosity, in essence the very soul of selflessness, is
sometimes brought under such insidious control by the
self that it becomes nothing more than the self's government surplus. Praise or condemnation for either
next-door neighbors or public figures is generally done
with such consummate skill that in either case it
amounts to some sort of promotion of one's self. When
I offer to tell you what I think of two presidential can-
didates, my real intention is often to tell you about
myself. Two former school acquaintances met after
some thirty years of separation. One of them had had a
brilliant career in music but unhappily he was both
insufferably conceited and tirelessly talkative. Without

stopping he spent an hour in praise of himself. Then he said, "Well, that's enough about me. Let's talk about you. How did *you* like my last recording?" This is how we love our self.

How gently subtle we are with our self! When it comes to ascribing motives, we have a positive genius for rationalization. Whatever the result of any of our actions, it always turns out that we had the right idea. If something went wrong, it must have been the fault of fate or friend or enemy. How dumb we are, to be so easily fooled. Of charity, Jesus said, "Do not let your left hand know what your right is doing." It seems an impossible admonition. Yet we accomplish something very like it all the time. We sin with either hand, and look the world coolly in the eye as though we had no idea what was going on. Even when we decide to castigate our self, beating our breast and crying, "Mea culpa!" it is always the *mea* that is emphasized. The self must be exhibited at any cost. Ted Williams is supposed to have said about the press, "I don't care what they say about me, as long as they keep talking about me." This is how we love our self.

In our secret imagination we are at our worst. The genius of James Thurber is proved by his ability to keep the story of Walter Mitty from running to twenty volumes. How conceited most of us are in the privacy of our hearts! For a considerable time in my youth I rode the New York subways every day. Automatically, as soon as I entered a car, I would look around for the most attractive looking young lady. And never, during those years, could I understand why these young ladies did not seem tempted to single me out for the same sort of fascinated attention which I so graciously offered them. Having failed to gain their attention with sheer good looks, I would then take out a book, the title carefully selected ahead of time—something about the philosophy of Thomas Aquinas or maybe even the Bible. Perhaps I could win them with my intellect. Failing that, I would ostentatiously get up and give my seat to an old lady. Gallantry! Maybe that would work. But, strangely, nothing ever came of my efforts.

An avid reader of the sports page in my younger days, I can still remember what a blow it was to me when the press began to report the feats of professional performers who were younger than I. It was hard for me to accept the fact that it was too late for me ever to become a professional athlete. But dreams of fame and achievement are not limited to youth. When Princeton University announced the election of Dr. Robert Goheen as its new president a few years ago, I was badly shaken for two weeks. I had had the pleasure of going to college with him, and was in fact a year ahead of him, and nobody had even bothered to ask me if I wanted the job. I didn't want it. The thought of being president of Princeton University had never occurred to me. I am totally and absolutely unqualified for the job. It was just that Walter Mitty had a dream, which he confesses now in print *as* a confession—but with the secret hope that readers will think it rather charming of him. The ego never rests. I am even a little annoyed at Mr. Thurber—if that is possible—for writing *The Secret Life Of Walter Mitty*. If he hadn't, I am perfectly sure I could have. That is how we love our self.

Some may argue that without the pride and self-confidence and ambition which are the fruit of self love, where would the world be? Do not most great

men have a large amount of self-esteem? And have not
these qualities been the very ones which have enabled
them to accomplish so much in the interests of mankind? If "Caesar was ambitious," was that really so bad
for his people and for the world? John W. Gardner, in
a book called *Excellence,* writes of people who achieve
distinction in any field, "Deep within them they have
a hard core of conviction and self trust that makes their
achievement possible." Leo Durocher expressed the
same idea less elegantly. "Nice guys finish last." It is a
hard thesis to find fault with, but I am not sure whether
this is due to its validity so much as to a confusion in
our modern minds as to what good is. In medieval times
the first of the seven deadly sins was pride; and high
on the list of the seven cardinal virtues was humility.
But in our day we simply don't believe that. For years
I have argued endlessly and fruitlessly about these concepts with young men in my classes. They are convinced that pride is a virtue. They were *taught* so. And
they are convinced that humility is a weakness. They
have inferred so.

On the plus side, perhaps one should give a little
ground. Surely some of the benefits to mankind (if we
do not quibble too much about what we mean by benefit) have been produced by cocky, self-assured, conceited, selfish, ambitious men. And, less offensively,
good has also come from men more charming in their
manner but still far too self-loving to be pleasing in
their inner souls to God. But, if pride is the author of
some good in the world, it is also the author of *all* evil
in the world. At least such is the contention of orthodox
Christian theologians. Thus, in the balance it must
stand condemned as a deadly sin.

Self

The chief thing wrong with pride is that it is a lie. Pride tells me that I am at the center of the universe, that everything must be measured—in distance, in attractiveness, and in goodness—by its relationship to me. I began to be aware of my central position the day I was born, and whether this view has been carefully nurtured or conscientiously combatted, it has persisted. But however dear it is to me, it is not so. I am not the center. God is.

I believe that there is no satisfactory answer to the problem of self that is not religious. And the religious answer is prayer. It is not a sure-fire answer, but it is the only possible one. It is not sure-fire because, even in the act of praying, it is no easy job to get rid of the self sufficiently to let God in. "God bless Mummy and Daddy" is, unfortunately, an insidious beginning to prayer, even though it has much tradition behind it. Why *my* Mummy and Daddy any more than anyone else's? "And make Johnny a good boy?" Well, all right; but, if Johnny were to learn to say, with all his heart, "Praise God, from whom all blessings flow; praise Him all creatures here below; praise Him above, ye heavenly host; praise Father, Son, and Holy Ghost," he would be well on the way to being a good boy—and his perspective would be better.

But, if "God bless Mummy and Daddy" is not the best of beginnings, it is at least a beginning. And however self-centered one's prayers may be, if they are prayers at all, they do at least give God a chance to clarify a few things in the worshipper's soul. *Eventually*, the person who prays is going to run out of things to say about himself and he may then move on to other topics. He may even stop talking altogether and try listening. In this context in particular, it is important to understand that prayer is not just an emotional out-pouring of the spirit—though it is that. It is also a discipline, and for that discipline there are aids available, like the Book of Common Prayer or the Missal, for example. Someone once asked Horace Taft, a Unitarian, which he preferred—the spontaneous prayers that come straight from the heart or the "canned prayers" of the Episcopal Church. He replied, "Oh, I much prefer the spontaneous prayers that come from the heart . . . until I hear one. Then I long for the beautiful language of the Book of Common Prayer." But it is not only the language, it is the subject matter. How many of us, left to our own devices, would get around to praying for Congress, or prisoners, or those in mental darkness or for schools and colleges? And who of us would think to offer simple prayers of *general* thanksgiving and praise? Yet, here lies the road to release from inordinate self-love. The middle of the Lord's Prayer is a self plea, but it is proper because it is surrounded at the beginning and the end by praise of God Almighty, for nothing except His Being.

Jesus was human, and so he once prayed, "My Father, if it is possible, let this cup pass me by." But even in his humanity he had a divine spark, and so he added, "Yet not as I will, but as thou wilt." Here the perspective is perfect. Here is the ground for believing the promise, "Ask, and you will receive; seek, and you will find; knock, and the door will be opened. For everyone who asks receives, he who seeks finds, and to him who knocks the door will be opened." This does not mean that you will necessarily receive what *you* want, or that you will find just what *you* are looking for, or that any door which happens to pique *your* curiosity will be opened. It does mean that if you are serious about "as thou wilt," there will be an answer, something will be found, some door opened. And always it will be as God wills. The acceptance of this one condition is the beginning of the end of inordinate self-love—not the permanent end, but at least a moment of truth. Then over and over the battle with self will begin again, though never will the struggle be quite so desperate as it was at the beginning since that first moment of truth will help to breed others.

If pride is a sin, its opposing virtue is humility, a concept, as already suggested, nearly as misunderstood in our day as its opposite. Nearly, because even though we do not hesitate to call pride a virtue, we are reluctant to call humility a sin. We just call it a weakness, a term which is hair-splitting, since that is the modern word for sin anyway. Unfortunately, our misunderstanding of humility is understandable. It has not generally enjoyed a good press. A familiar hymn contains the lines, "Strip me of the robe of pride; clothe me with humility." The poetic figure brings to mind a picture of a disgraced army officer being drummed out of the corps, his insignia and medals removed in public disgrace. That God is doing the drumming out (if that *is* the situation), that I know full well that the charges are just, that I apparently asked for punishment by confessing my sins freely—these circumstances still do not make me feel drawn toward humility as a virtue. If this is what humility really is, then the religion is harsh which demands it as a cardinal virtue.

But I do not believe that the picture here drawn is at all the true nature of humility. It is more like humiliation. I believe that humility, in the Christian sense, is something quite different. To begin with, I think the robe of pride was stolen. It belonged to humility in the first place. True humility is regal. It is no beggar, in beggars' rags. When we come upon it, we know we are in the presence of greatness, the kind of unobtrusive greatness which makes us feel pleasantly warm and at ease. There is no display, no glamour, no high-sounding names or titles. Humility comes quietly into the room, while pride is talking. The robe it wears is neither a hair shirt nor a garment of striking splendor. Its beauty and distinction are simply that it fits very well. When humility speaks to us, it invariably hits upon our favorite subject—ourselves. And so we are entranced at once. Only afterwards, because of the warmth and ease within us, do we chance to ask, "Who was that fascinating man I spoke with?" "Don't you know?" replies a friend. "That was Humility, a very great man." Yes, a very great man indeed. We were not conscious of the greatness as we spoke with him, but now it dawns on us.

I know a man who is filled with such humility. Now retired from an active career, his accomplishments have been such as to make him universally known, respected, and revered in his profession. Yet he is not famous outside that field, so in most social gatherings it is easy for him to be unobtrusive. Except for his passionate and wholly engaging interest in all people and his contagious enthusiasm for life, he might never be noticed in a crowd at all. It also happens that he is the most incurable optimist I have ever known. Whether that fact is allied to his humility or not is another matter and a most interesting one. But for the moment let it just be treated as an extraneous extra bit of information.

At a dinner party once I happened to be seated near

this friend. At his right was an elderly and charming lady but a lady of rather strong opinions freely expressed. I was engaged in conversation elsewhere, but I am a practiced, inveterate, and highly skilled eavesdropper. I heard the lady say to my friend, "I am an incurable pessimist. I always think the worst is going to happen." I was not surprised that he already had her talking of herself, but I had a sudden sinking feeling that my friend—the incurable optimist, the humblest of men and among the most gallant too—would not be able to get himself out of this conversational trap. His response was instantaneous and vigorous. "So am I!" he said. "Except on occasion. And this, dear lady, is such an occasion!"

One of the hardest things in the world to sacrifice is an opinion, a point of view, perhaps because it is so close to one's ego. And how my friend must have wanted to take up the cudgels and argue with that lady. His optimism means so much to him, is so much a part of his life and his whole being. But his humility means more. So he agreed with her, or at least seemed to. And it did so much for the old lady to have his assurance that she was right. Of course, my friend's optimism carried the day anyway, for in spite of the dour convictions of the lady, the conversation turned out to be one of the gayest I have ever overheard.

Such is the nature of true humility. It is gay. It is light-hearted. It is delightful. Having conquered its only bitter enemy—the self—life becomes for it one long and magnificent victory celebration. Whenever humility rules the heart there is laughter, the most graceful laughter in all the world, the laughter of sheer joy. Humor is its first cousin. Not ridicule or derision but

pure humor. Someone has said that a sense of humor is
nothing more than a sense of proportion. And to achieve
a sense of proportion, nothing needs to be put in its
proper place so desperately as one's self. Humility does
that for humor. The laughter that follows is clean.

I have said earlier that courage makes other virtues
possible. Humility does not merely make them possible;
it gives birth to them. Just as pride is the source of
other sins, so humility is the source of other virtues
—of charity, of generosity, of honor, for example. None
of these is possible until one's self has been set aside.
Humility subdues one's self, and thus suddenly brings
other virtues within reach. Humility is a prize, a charming and rewarding way of life.

How is this prize achieved? Obviously it is not easy,
or there would be much more humility in the world
than there is. In his first Epistle, St. Peter suggests a
way. In writing to the elders of various churches, he
at first suggests that the elders take the lead, take
charge of things, and that the younger people submit
to that lead. Then he seems to have a change of heart
and adds, "Indeed, all of you should wrap yourselves
in the garment of humility towards each other." It is,
it would seem, an act of the will. The suggestion is not
that we be humble because our place in life is lowly
but that we be humble no matter what our position is
and specifically that we be humble before our fellow
man, no matter what *his* position. "All of you . . .
towards each other."

Once when I was attending a three-day educational
conference, I came down to the hotel dining room for
breakfast on the day of departure and was ushered to
a table for four where three men were already seated.

Self

Two of them I knew, and they promptly introduced me to the third, who turned out to be the then newly elected president of Harvard University, Dr. Nathan Pusey. A quick glance at everyone's plate revealed that my two friends were almost finished breakfast and were, as it happened, rushing to catch a train. Dr. Pusey, on the other hand, was just starting, and in panic I realized that I was about to have breakfast *alone* with this great man in the world of education. What on earth should I talk about? One whimsical thought flitted quickly across my mind—an "inside" small school trade joke: "Well, Dr. Pusey, how's your enrollment this year?" I discarded it. My alarm was, of course, unnecessary for Dr. Pusey's grace saved the day. He immediately began asking me questions about my school, and so I had a delightful time. I went away feeling quite wonderful. And, virtue being its own reward, perhaps he did too.

It may be that such a story makes humility sound more like a technique than a virtue, even tinged with a bit of hypocrisy. Perhaps so, but the Devil uses techniques, knowing that by such methods souls may sometimes be won to him. So, too, may souls be won to virtue. If one were to start practicing humility only as a technique, one might begin to discover that it is more. Jesus himself said, "When you receive an invitation, go and sit down in the lowest place." Perhaps we must begin with our fellow man, any man who happens to come along, for to select only those who are obviously superior is but a feeble gesture toward humility. One may call the conscious practice of humility a technique. One may call it an amenity, or even a game. But as athletic games are good for the body, so too, may such

a game as this be good for the soul. I admit that it is
not as simple as I make it sound. But a little beginning,
a modest beginning, even a frivolous beginning, may
lead we know not where.

Naturally St. Peter did not stop with urging all people to show humility toward each other. Almost in the
same breath he said, "Humble yourselves then under
God's mighty hand." Of course the soul and the source
of humility, is humility before God. From a logical
standpoint, the relationship to God ought to be the
starting point. Men of great pride and mighty wills, like
Job and St. Paul and St. Augustine, learned humility
only through a staggering and dramatic confrontation
directly with the voice of God Almighty. They were, so
to speak, beaten into submission by God Himself. Only
then could they go out into the world, meeting whom-
ever they might meet, and subject themselves one to
another, wrapped "in the garment of humility."

For most of us, however, I suspect the way is different. We are more likely to succeed by following the
pattern of St. Augustine's mother, Monica, or Ruth, or
St. Francis, first subjecting ourselves to our fellow men,
however gently, however gingerly. Whatever hints of
truth we may so acquire we may bring into Church
with us of a Sunday morning and discover that they
are strangely relevant to our worship, that they have a
spiritual dimension of which we never knew, that they
do indeed help us to be humble "under God's mighty
hand."

So pernicious and devastating is the ego rampant,
and so delightful is life when the ego is properly humbled, that it is hard to imagine many goals more desirable for a man than the control of his self and its

inordinate self-affection. It is hard to imagine, too, how this can better be achieved than through religious faith. By the very nature of the problem, one is so tangled and involved and confused with himself that a solution seems hopeless without some help from the outside. The self within is like the hands in that old game in which one's fingers are so intricately intertwined that it becomes difficult to move the specific finger one is asked to move. To attempt to solve the riddle of one's self without help is like a knot trying to untie itself. Alone, the more one thinks about the problem of getting his self in proper perspective, the more he tends to meet his self coming around the corner.

In my mind there is no doubt, that true humility is best achieved and the self most neatly contained by men who believe. Their faith is at once their pride's check and their humility's strength. They are thus twice rewarded; indeed, three times, the last by grace. "If a great king wished to send his daughter to some place," wrote Brother Giles, one of the "Little Flowers" of St. Francis, "he would not put her on an untamed, proud, and stubborn horse, but on a gentle horse that was easy to ride—so the Lord does not bestow His grace on the proud but on the humble."

Church

I have said and said again that this is not a book about *how* to believe but about why. Why believe? Because faith works. In discussions of a variety of the most common human situations, I have tried to demonstrate that faith is relevant, that it is helpful, that people who have it are better off than people who do not. More precisely, I mean to say that the extent to which one has it (for I doubt that there is any such thing as a person without any faith at all) one is helped. Still more specifically, I have tried to point out that those whose faith is expressed in, and finds it source within, the framework of some traditional, historic, formal religion are better served in most human situations than the rest of the world.

The modern mass media experts might say that the trouble with the Gospel is that it is *good* news, and everybody knows that good news is no news. What fascinates most of us is bad news, and consequently that is what we are generally fed by those who sell news. My hope here is to call some attention to the news of goodness, to get people to look around them with a little more care and see if there are not some people in the world who have a few particularly helpful and winsome answers to the perplexities of life. In the final analysis, I do not think I can tell anyone how such people got that way. My goal is simply to try to get some of the rest of the world to say, "I wish I knew," and mean it. When someone sits down at a party and starts to play the piano, others are likely to say, "I wish I could play like that." But they don't really mean it with all their hearts. If they did, most of them could learn to "play like that." In the realm of faith, we need to wish with a little more passion. If we did, then I think we would be on the road to finding out how it might be achieved. Because I believe that the honest desire to believe precedes all else, I have concentrated here almost exclusively on the question of why.

I admit, however, that the two questions how and why are interrelated and that one cannot and should not ignore the former altogether. For one thing, it is in the area of *how* that one usually finds out the price tag. For example, it would be easy to persuade most people that they ought to have two cars. There are a thousand convincing answers to the question why. But the reason so many people still do not have a second car is that they haven't found the answer to how it is to be acquired—how the down payment and the subsequent installments are to be made, what other things are to be sacrificed for it.

I have already touched on the subject of how to believe. In the chapter on Love I tried to suggest a part of an answer to the question of how one can believe. At that point I discussed emotion. Here let us approach the question from a different direction, this time in terms of a program. But for the final time I do want to emphasize that I still do not consider this question of how to believe the primary one. If, instead of a second car, the question is why (with peritonitis) should I have my appendix out, the answer to that question— why—is likely to be so persuasive that no difficulties about how are apt to stand in the way. It is a matter of life and death. *Ideally*, it is only in such a spirit—when faith has become an urgent necessity, or a matter of deep yearning—that the question, "How can I believe?" can be asked with any hope of finding a satisfactory answer.

How essential a yearning is can be illustrated by the nature of the answer I have to suggest. It is, simply, *join the Church*. That answer is so time-worn and shop-worn; and there are so many things wrong with the Church that at the very outset all cynics and many skeptics will immediately drop out of line right here from sheer boredom. To them I am tempted to say, "You didn't really want to learn to play the piano." Or, "You know perfectly well you don't need two cars." And to some I might even want to say, "Don't you know people die of peritonitis?" Joining the Church is not a new and glamorous idea, but it is the beginning of the answer.

It needs, I well know, a great deal of explanation and defense even for those whose hearts are filled with yearning. The first objection is a legitimate one: "But if I don't believe, how can I join? Don't they ask you to believe as a condition of joining? Don't you have to make all sorts of vows that an honest man couldn't pos-

sibly make unless he *already* believed everything the
Church might in time bring him to believe?"

There can be no denying that there is truth in this
objection, but the truth exists more in theory than in
practice. At issue is the basic question of conscience
and commitment. Think, for a moment, in terms of
patriotism. During the past century millions of people
from every corner of the earth have come to America
to make it their permanent home. Before their arrival
they had only the vaguest idea of all that America stood
for, and usually that idea could have been expressed
as a generality like freedom or opportunity. Not all,
but most of those who have adopted America as their
new home have become good citizens, some very great
citizens. Little by little, as they have committed themselves (indeed exactly to the extent that they have committed themselves), they have come to an ever
deepening understanding and belief. Along with the
good, they have found things they could not accept,
things that have disappointed them, and things that
they have felt called upon vigorously to oppose. Only
very rarely, however, have such disappointments re-
sulted in a lessening of their patriotism. On the contrary, it is often on the basis of patriotism that the
objections are made.

Theoretically, I suppose, one ought not to join any
organization or institution without first knowing all
about it. In practice, however, this nearly impossible
condition is replaced by an interaction that develops
between the person and the organization. Of course
there has to be some initial attraction, some first appeal
to one's ideals and conscience and needs. But the deep-

est and fullest range of belief comes only *after* the commitment is made.

This interaction, this developing relationship, is a common experience. It is seen in marriage, for example. It is rare that parents of brides and grooms are persuaded that "they know each other well enough." But memories of parents are short. The fact is that brides and grooms have never known each other well enough to have been able to make the fantastic vows they are asked to make. It is just not possible. One has to be married for years before he can hope to know a mate well enough to judge whether or not he would like to live with him or her the rest of their lives. And the more "sensible" people are in trying to overcome this difficulty, the less likely they are to succeed. "Some enchanted evening" is still as good a way to introduce one to a life-long commitment to his mate as any other.

There has to be a little daring in life, a little adventurousness, a little faith. Those who say that they have remained outside the Church for conscience's sake are too often deluding themselves about the reason. Their consciences are just not that sensitive in other areas of life, and the *self* that they are so hesitant to commit to anything that might order it about a bit is not all that precious.

As with marriage and patriotism, so with the Church. Of course there has to be that initial spark of attraction. That, in one sense, is what this book is all about. But given that spark, there is no reason why countless uncommitted people could not make the commitment out of which a firmer and more articulate and precise and powerful belief may gradually emerge. There simply is no way that faith can be acquired ahead of time from the outside. And within the Church there is still ample room for doubt and questioning and for a fair amount of private opinion. There is no convincing evidence that those who have made such a commitment through the centuries have on the whole been weaker-willed, less devoted to conscience or less intelligent than those who have refused.

A second common objection to joining the Church is somewhat harder to answer than the first. The objector simply points to the many sorry chapters in the history of the Church, the crimes it has committed and the crimes it has condoned by silence: the Inquisition, the crusades, the persecution of the Jews in times both ancient and modern, its foot-dragging on crucial racial issues at home and abroad, the witch hunts now and in the past. "Why" says the skeptic, "why should I join an organization with a record as besmirched as that?"

It must be admitted that whenever the Church has functioned as a political entity, it has committed all the crimes of other political entities and by its claims of sanctity made them all a little worse. But the Church was never supposed to be a political entity, and whenever it has abstained from that the record has been better. The accusation here is simply that the Church has not yet succeeded in saving either the world or its own soul or the souls of its own. That is true.

But if the sweep of human history reveals anything that might be called moral and spiritual progress—and I believe it does reveal such, not as a steady upswing, but as an upswing nevertheless—I believe that progress can usually be traced to some ideal or principle or some particular instance of strong individual leadership which has its origin in the Church. (Here I would most em-

phatically like to include more than the Christian
Church. The record of Judaism, for example, is probably the brightest of all religious groups.) There is no
other kind of human institution which has anything like
as firm a claim, no government, no philosophy, not even
the whole mainstream of secular learning. And speaking of secular learning, is not the record of science, for
example, as besmirched with unholiness—even by its
own measure of what is unholy—as that of the Church?
Yet good men do not therefore say, "Because of the
sins committed in its name, we shall eschew science."
The Christian Church has existed for two thousand
years for the express purpose of serving the moral and
spiritual well-being of the world. Other churches have
lived longer, for the same purpose. No other kinds of
human institutions have existed for any thing like as
long for such exalted goals. Over the centuries, the
Church has many times lost sight of its high purpose.
But it has also demonstrated a striking capacity eventually to purge itself and return to its appointed tasks.

There is still a third objection to joining the Church.
It is more common than either of the first two, but
easier to answer. The charge is hypocrisy. "I look at the
Church, and all I see is a bunch of hypocrites," says
the critic. "I know So-and-so. I see him at work every
day of the work week and I know what kind of a man
he really is. How has he got the *nerve* to show up in
church on Sunday? And to pass the plate! As for Mrs.
So-and-so, she just goes to be seen, or rather to show
off her wardrobe."

Of course there are hypocrites in the Church. But
I really think this is no reason at all for not joining. In
the first place, while I am sure hypocrites do exist in

the Church, I would hate to point my finger and say, "There goes one now." Hypocrisy is probably the most intimate and secret sin there is. Nobody on earth can know who is a hypocrite except himself and God, and sometimes not even himself. All hypocrites are sinners, to be sure, but all sinners are not hypocrites. Mr. So-and-so may know better than anyone else that he is a sinner and he may be going to church on Sundays in the desperate hope that he may *become* a better man during the rest of the week. The process may take a lifetime, and all the time the man must certainly look like a hypocrite to the rest of the world. But who is to say that in his heart he really is? And *who*, pray tell, has the slightest idea why Mrs. So-and-so goes to church? Ascribing motives to other people is a dangerous game. I myself don't really know why I go to church. I know what I think are the reasons, and what I hope are the reasons, but I dare not go farther than that.

In the second place, surely it is blind (maybe even hyprocritical) to suppose that one can avoid association with hypocrites by staying away from church. They exist outside as well as in. Again one must try to avoid pointing an accusing finger in any one direction. Still, if I were God, and if I were looking for hypocrites, I might start with those who say, "The reason I don't go to church is because I prefer to worship God alone, in my own way." I have never met anyone who has taken that stand who has not eventually revealed one way or another that he really prefers not to worship God at all. He does not prefer to eat alone, or to sleep alone, or to work alone, or even to go on vacation alone. Strange that he should only want to worship alone—

and in his own way, with no acknowledgement of debt to his religious forebears. This is not to say that there is not a place, a very important place, in all world religions for private devotions. They are not merely permitted; they are essential. But such cannot be a substitute for corporate worship, nor has it often existed except within the framework of the Church, its literature, its liturgies, and its traditions.

What is the Church? Someone once divided religion into three parts—believing, behaving, and belonging. Except for its initial appeal, the catching of the eye of the potential member either through the belief or the behavior of the committed, the Church is first and foremost belonging. By belonging, the committed person comes constantly to deeper and more satisfying beliefs and ever more worthy patterns of behavior. Primarily the Church means belonging. Whatever else it means follows from that. In the Christian Church this belonging is expressed both as a concept or ideal, and as a specific institution, a reality on this earth.

In Holy Scripture there are many phrases and figures of speech to describe the concept of the Church—the Holy Catholic Church, the Communion of Saints, the Kingdom of God on earth, the Body of Christ. The last, perhaps the most difficult to understand and accept, may also prove the most helpful. At first this figure of speech seems confusing and inappropriate, and certainly archaic. How could the Church—a thing so imperfect, so beset with divisions and sins—be in any way equated with Him, whom some call the Son of God? Is it not an insult to Him?

In search of understanding, perhaps we should consider the word quite literally. What is the function of a

Church

body? What can it do? What is it unable to do? A human being is, of course, not simply a body. It is a spirit—a combination of hopes and fears, of generosity and selfishness, of ambition and lethargy, of love and hate, of honesty and dishonesty, of security and insecurity—all spiritual qualities, none having to do with the body. Details of height and weight and coloring tell us nothing of these spiritual qualities. Nevertheless, the body is not unimportant. Only through it does the spirit become available to other people. So true is this that, rightly or wrongly, we promote the notion that *some* physical descriptions *do* reveal something of the spirit. We speak of a weak chin, or an open face, or a frank expression, or a clear eye, of a resolute or irresolute step.

It is hard for us to recall the spirit unless the body is present. When we do succeed in capturing in our minds the spirit of one who is physically absent, it is by recollecting what he looks like. My mother died twenty-five years ago. I loved her and still love her very much indeed, but I am shamed by the fact that I have trouble remembering what she *looked* like. What is worse still, this means that I have trouble remembering what she *was* like. I need reminders—mementos, old letters with the words she wrote to me, pictures, and the testimony of others who knew her. Some time ago I went to England and visited places where she had been. That helped too, even though I had never been there with her. Such outward and physical things are not the person. They are not even the spirit. They are merely media through which a person's spirit is made available. The body itself, in its most literal sense, is gone and now irrelevant. These associated things now

214

Church

are the body. It is in some such literal sense that I believe the words of St. Paul are to be interpreted—"the Church, which is the body of Christ."

Peculiar to the Christian faith is the unique opportunity to know God rather precisely through His Son. For the original disciples this must have been an incredibly exciting experience—to know God through daily personal association with Jesus Christ, to eat with Him and speak with Him and walk with Him and be taught by Him. But as a man on this earth He has been dead now for two thousand years. So for the rest of us He cannot be known as He was by those first disciples. To some extent we have to say that He has slipped away from us.

Still, we do have the Church, and in it are mementos and symbols: a cross, the symbol of His suffering and of His victory; a baptismal font; an altar; a pulpit—each reminiscent of some aspect of His life. In the Church have been recorded and preserved words, meaningful, helpful words, which He uttered. There are sacraments and rituals and ceremonies—the commemoration of the Last Supper, the laying on of hands, special services of healing. Also, in the name of Jesus Christ the Church performs certain functions—social service, particular witness to truth and beauty. And finally, the Church is the repository of the testimony and witness of many thousands of people for centuries past who have, each in his own way, known this man.

For us this is the body of Christ. It is not Christ himself, and surely it is not His spirit. But without it how could He be known to us? Often, as I have already suggested, the Church is indeed a poor and feeble thing as a vehicle for the spirit of Jesus. A friend of mine once stood beside the hospital bed of an elderly, dying lady, holding her hand. She was very old and after years of illness her body was a pitiful thing—so worn out, so desperately inadequate to contain her magnificent spirit. "I can hardly wait to get out of this loathsome body of mine," she said. She had not long to wait. Yet after even that most inadequate body was gone, her spirit too began to slip away a little. Surely the Church is most inadequate to preserve the spirit of Jesus Christ. But we have nothing better. Those who would believe cannot afford to scorn it or avoid it or neglect it. They must belong.

Those who are already professing Christians ought to be able to agree with what has been said so far. Theirs is a church religion, and the Church cannot be separated from their faith, since it is so deeply rooted in it. One person's interpretation may differ in numerous details from another's, but the basic concept is central to what all Christians believe. (Those who maintain that a man can be as good a Christian apart from the Church as from within it deny the validity of their position by the very ignorance of Christian teaching which their argument displays.) It is not the Church as a *concept* which is the stumbling block for most of us. It is particular institutions that we object to. Here is where the inadequacies and inconsistencies and so-called hypocrisies begin to show up. "The Church" may be the "Body of Christ," but it is also the particular parish nearest to your home or mine, with whatever beauty and whatever violations of beauty, whatever harmony and whatever disharmony, whatever competence and whatever incompetence it may contain.

The Church is a very comfortable and fashionable

city parish, a beautiful French Gothic cathedral, a
poverty-stricken mission parish somewhere in the back
country, a strife-ridden small-town church. It is the
silo-shaped M.I.T. chapel, the so-called "fish church"
of Stamford, Connecticut, and the new cathedral at
Coventry. It is a bare Quaker meeting house and a city
temple that looks like an apartment house. It is a center
aisle worn with a thousand years of worshippers' feet
and it is the latest thing in multi-colored asphalt tile.
It is plush cushions for easy kneeling. It is rigid straight
benches for hard sitting. It is a high altar with a light
and a reserved sacrament. It is altarless, with a pulpit in
the middle, an honest hour glass attached. The Church
is a preacher of eloquent persuasiveness, a pastor of
uncommon compassion, a scholar of impressive learning. It is also a poor pitiful parson, by learning and
talent and personality truly incapable of properly per-
forming any of the tasks assigned to him. It is an ego-
maniac, a menace marauding as a man of God. It is a
true saint. It is one of the world's greatest organists
playing a fabulous instrument in a famous cathedral.
It is a talentless local schoolteacher, pounding out
hymns on a cheap pump organ because she is the only
one in town who can read a little music. It is the ma-
jestic music of a Bach chorale. It is the saccharine-sweet
sentimental music of Nineteenth-Century revivalism.
The Church is liturgy—sometimes with dignity and
sometimes without.

Always the Church is people—in the pulpit, at the
organ, in the choir, on vestries, in the congregation—
people sometimes magnificent, sometimes sinful. Most
of them are acceptable people in most ways most of
the time. But in the Church they often disappoint us

simply because there we somehow expect them to be different. When they are not, we are discouraged and disillusioned. What really upsets us is not the doctrine of the Resurrection of the Body but the way our own minister reads the prayers; not the doctrine of the Trinity but the every-member canvass; not the doctrine of Original Sin but the ineptitude of our child's Sunday-school teacher. The Church as the Body of Christ is a noble concept, but when we get down to cases we are disheartened by incompetence, inadequacy, and pettiness.

Still the believer must belong. He has no choice, if he would believe. For with all its sins, weaknesses, and imperfections—yes, precisely with them—the Church has incredible strength and virtue and moral and spiritual force. More than any other human institution, it contains within itself the source and means of its own purification, reform, and revitalization. Out of its weakness has come strength over and over again in its history. Those who have thought to use it to their own ends have learned to fear it or have been cleansed by it. There is decay and death in the Church, but there is also always new life. It is from the Church that have come the Augustines, Francises, Aquinases, John XXIII's, Luthers, Wesleys, Temples, Bailies, and Tillichs, and countless others, saints and spiritual giants, some famous and some not. Nor have they come simply from "The Church, the Body of Christ," but from inadequate little parishes perhaps worse than yours and mine, led and populated by little people, beset by the disheartening sins of little people, but parishes to which these great souls *belonged* and made better—and were made better *by* belonging.

Church

To those outside the Church who have read this far, and who now say, in effect, "What you say sounds good. And you know I really would like to believe. I am sure it must be better. But I just can't. How do I go about it?", I say join the Church, which of course means join a church.

I say further that you may expect miracles. They do happen. But do not expect only miracles, and don't expect the way to faith to be easy or quick. As we look with envy at the rewards gathered by so many of the faithful, we need to remember the long hard road traversed by them, that led them to their faith. Abraham "believed God and it was accounted unto him for righteousness." But Abraham, in his bewildering search, went through the agony of thinking that he would have to sacrifice his own son and very nearly did. When Moses came down from Mount Sinai, having communed directly with God on the subject of righteousness, "the skin of his face shone because he had been talking with God." But his people had to wander through the wilderness for forty years before they were ushered into the Promised Land. Even then, for his sins, Moses himself was not allowed to enter, though he must have understood something about the significance of the Promised Land which those who entered never did understand. Long before God had said to him, "Put off thy shoes from off thy feet, for the place whereon thou standest is holy ground." Elijah had spent forty days and forty nights praying in a cave in the wilderness before he heard the "still small voice." Even Jesus Himself was not spared, but "was led up by the Spirit into the wilderness to be tempted by the Devil. And he fasted forty days and forty nights, and afterwards he was hungry."

If the recurring number forty is symbolic, it is not *merely symbolic*. Those two words do not go together. The truth is that in each case the trials lasted a long time, a very long time, and they were hard times. There were no quick and easy answers. And the recurrence of the word "wilderness" is no coincidence either, for that is precisely where one must wander if one is to find faith. Without faith, or before faith, there is no other place to wander. In that wilderness the Church is not an oasis, but neither is it a mirage. It is a chart, showing the way but guaranteeing nothing about that way except that it need no longer be aimless. Along the route, the Church also gives encouragement and strength. At the end of Jesus' time in the wilderness, after His temptations, it is recorded, "Then the devil left him, and behold, angels came and ministered to him." After Him, that has been the experience of many.

*   *   *

In the search for faith there is perhaps no more comprehensive story than the story of the Transfiguration and the account which immediately follows it in St. Mark's Gospel. It starts with Jesus taking just three of his disciples with him "up a high mountain apart by themselves." The three were Peter and James and John, perhaps the three closest to Him. There on the top of the mountain a miracle took place. They saw a vision and heard a voice. The vision was of Jesus and Moses and Elijah, all talking together. The appearance of

Jesus was completely transfigured. They had never seen Him so before. They were so overcome that they did not know what to do. The impetuous Peter blurted out something. " 'Master; it is well that we are here; let us make three booths, one for you and one for Moses and one for Elijah.' For he did not know what to say, for they were exceedingly afraid." Just then a cloud appear and a voice came out of the cloud. "This is my beloved Son; listen to him."

In our search for faith, this is the sort of high drama we long for; and in our impatience we are likely to find fault with God and say, in effect, "If He would just do something like that for me, I'd believe too." But we need to remember that these were disciples, men who had already committed themselves to Jesus, whom Peter called "Master," and who had been with Him night and day for weeks and months. We need to remember too that they were specially selected disciples, not all twelve, but only three. They were holy men, such as we are not. We have no more right to expect insights such as theirs than we have to expect insights such as Albert Einstein's.

When Jesus and the three who were with Him came down from the mountain to join the other disciples, they saw a great crowd gathered. When He asked what the discussion was about, one of the crowd answered, "Teacher, I brought my son to you, for he has a dumb spirit; and wherever it seizes him, it dashes him down; and he foams and grinds his teeth and becomes rigid; and I asked your disciples to cast it out, and they were not able." Presumably it was to His own disciples, the nine who had remained at the foot of the mountain, that He said, "O faithless generation, how long am I to be with you?" It seemed that even those nine, holy men as we are not, had not all the answers to the problems of faith. Still, there was a great promise to come.

Jesus questioned the man, who, after describing his son's condition a little more fully, cried, "But if you can do anything, have pity on us and help us." This clearly was the agonized cry of a man who knew that he was in trouble and was desperate for help wherever he could find it. He must have heard somewhere of Jesus' healing powers and in his suffering for his son decided to seek Him out. Obviously his faith was not crystal clear; there was some doubt, nurtured a little, unfortunately, by the failure of the disciples to help him. So his opening words were hardly winning in their confidence. "If you can do anything." . . . It is neither unfair nor ungracious, therefore, that the beginning of Jesus' answer should be nothing but an echo. "If you can!" Furthermore, in this phrase lies the very crux of the whole matter of the efficacy of faith. The unbeliever can cry all he wants to about the unfairness of God in "giving some people the gift of faith" and withholding it from others, as though it were in no way connected with human will. But there *is* a connection. God has to have something to work with, not much at the start, but something. This man was desperate, and there is some reason to suspect the faith born of such desperation. But at least he did come to Jesus, he did call Him "Teacher," and in other accounts he got down on his knees before Him, and, if he still had doubts, they were ingratiatingly honest doubts. So he got an answer.

Though Jesus started with an echo, a throwing back of responsibility into the man's own lap, He followed it with the most glorious promise from God to man. "All things are possible to him who believes." Deeply moved, but still honest about his doubts, the man cried out just five words that could well be engraved on the heart of anyone truly concerned about the struggle for faith. "I believe; help my unbelief!" And Jesus did that.

The initial venture of faith—the first beginning, some small preliminary knuckling under of self-will, a grain of humility, a tentative offer of trust—must come from man. God meets man much more than halfway. He offers him everything—except faith. That is man's offering to God, and actually it is all he has to offer. The man whose complaint is, "I'd really like to believe, but I just can't bring myself to it" has said perhaps more than he meant to. As he ventures out of the house in search of faith, he leaves his self behind. It is so precious to him that he keeps it at home, safely locked up. That's not God's fault. The key is in that man's pocket, not God's. In the final analysis he must face a hard answer. "All things are not possible to you because you refuse to believe." At last, I do not see how that word "refuse" can be avoided.

In all that has been written here I have not meant to imply that life for the faithful is always easy, that there is no pain or suffering or disappointment or bewilderment. Moses suffered and so did Job and so did the Son of God Himself. Faith is not an easy answer to all of the problems of life. It is a very hard answer. Doubt is never completely defeated, even in the hearts of the most saintly. And, whenever doubt holds sway for an hour or a day or a year, the experience of the prophets of Baal recurs; there is no voice; no one answers; no one heeds.

Church

But, if faith is not an easy answer, it *is* an answer, and a good one. In the lives of believers—not only in centuries past but today—there is an abundance of evidence that faith works, which I find very convincing.